Thomas Arnold

Fragment on the Church

Thomas Arnold

Fragment on the Church

ISBN/EAN: 9783743349940

Manufactured in Europe, USA, Canada, Australia, Japa

Cover: Foto ©ninafisch / pixelio.de

Manufactured and distributed by brebook publishing software (www.brebook.com)

Thomas Arnold

Fragment on the Church

FRAGMENT

ON

THE CHURCH.

THIRD EDITION:

IN WHICH ARE CONTAINED

APPENDICES ON THE SAME SUBJECT.

BY

THOMAS ARNOLD, D.D.

LATE HEAD MASTER OF RUGBY SCHOOL.

LONDON:
T. FELLOWES, LUDGATE STREET.
1863.

LONDON:
R. CLAY, SON, AND TAYLOR, PRINTERS,
BREAD STREET HILL.

ADVERTISEMENT.

The following pages, chiefly composed in 1839, 40, 41, are a part of a much longer work which Dr. Arnold contemplated, but which was interrupted by his early death.

The executors having kindly allowed me to fulfil my wishes as to this fragment, I have felt it a duty not to withhold what remains from his pen on the subject which so greatly occupied his thoughts.

The earlier approaches to the same subject it has been thought desirable, even at the risk of some inconvenience to the purchasers of the first edition, to publish in the form of Appendices to the fragment of 1839, 40. The brief sketches of 1827, 1833, and 1840, may be useful in showing how very small a portion of the Author's design was actually accomplished in the following pages; whilst the fragments of 1833 may illustrate a portion of the argument which accidentally he had treated of more fully in his earlier than his later MSS. on the subject.

I have been entirely indebted to Mr. Stanley for the whole arrangement and revision of the present volume.

MARY ARNOLD.

Fox How, March 25, 1845.

THE CHURCH.

CHAPTER I.

THE language of prophecy leads us to hope for more than the salvation of a certain number of individuals through the Gospel. It speaks of a general restoration, so complete as to repair altogether the mischief which had been introduced into the world by sin. And the language of St. Paul, when declaring the great mystery of his preaching, namely, the admission of the Gentiles into the kingdom of God, seems also to go beyond the redemption of a few individuals, comparatively speaking, out of the multitude of all nations. Christ was to present unto himself a Church holy and without blemish; and the distinction made by some between the visible and invisible Church, seems only a later refinement of interpretation, suggested by the fact that the Church, in the obvious sense of the term, was not pure and spotless. Now, ought we to lower the language of prophecy, in order to make it agree with the existing state of things, or to be anxious to amend the existing state of things, for the very reason that it does not correspond with the promises of Scripture?

The spread of Christianity, speaking of the geographical extent of its mere nominal dominion, has been partial;—its real moral effects have been still more partial. The largest part of the world does not acknowledge Christ so much as in name; and where he is acknowledged in name, he is yet denied in many instances in works. The perfect work of the Gospel has been seen only in individuals; Christ has laid his hands on a few sick folk and healed them; but he has done no mighty work of spiritual healing on a whole church. It is still most true, that we see not yet all things put under him.

Now, are we prepared to say that, whereas the world was lost by one man's sin, it was only to be in a small part recovered by one man's righteousness?—that, whereas through Adam all died, only a very small number were through Christ to be made alive? This is directly contrary to the language of Scripture, which represents the redemption as designed to be a full reparation of the evil occasioned by the fall.

Or are we prepared to say that God's purposes have been defeated by the greater power of God's enemy?—that sin has been stronger than grace, Satan mightier than Christ?—that the Church with its Divine Head and its indwelling Spirit has

been unable to overcome the powers of evil?
—that the medicine was too weak to overcome
the disease?

If neither of these alternatives be true; if the
Scripture will not allow us to doubt of God's
gracious will towards us all; and if to doubt his
power be blasphemy,—what remains, but that we
have weakened and corrupted that medicine, which
was in itself sufficient to heal us?—that we have
not tried, and are not trying Christianity, such as
Christ willed it to be?—that the Church, against
which the powers of hell have so long maintained
an advantageous conflict, cannot be that same
Church against which Christ declared that they
should not prevail?

Now here it is necessary, in order to prevent
much confusion and very much uncharitableness,
to distinguish carefully between what I may be
allowed to call Christian religion and the Christian
Church.[a].

By Christian religion, I mean that knowledge of
God and of Christ, and that communion of the
Holy Spirit, by which an individual is led through
life, in all holiness, and dies with the confident
hope of rising again through Christ at the last
day. This knowledge being derived, or derivable
at any rate, from the Scriptures alone, and this
communion being the answer to our earnest

[a] [See Serm. xxxix. in vol. iv.; Lect. on Modern Hist. vi.]

prayers, it is perfectly possible that Christian religion may work its full work on an individual living alone, or living amongst unbelieving or ungodly men,—that here, where the business rests only with God and the individual soul, God's glory may be exalted and the man's salvation effected, whatever may be the state of the Church at large.

But, by the Christian Church, I mean that provision for the communicating, maintaining, and enforcing of this knowledge by which it was to be made influential, not on individuals, but on masses of men. This provision consisted in the formation of a society, which by its constitution should be capable of acting both within itself and without; having, so to speak, a twofold movement, the one for its outward advance, the other for its inward life and purification; so that Christianity should be at once spread widely and preserved the while in its proper truth and vigour, till Christian knowledge should be not only communicated to the whole world, but be embraced also in its original purity, and bring forth its practical fruit. Thus Christian religion and the Christian Church being two distinct things, the one acting upon individuals, the other upon masses; it is very possible for the former to continue to do its work, although the latter be perverted or disabled. But then the consequence will be such as we see before us, that Christianity, being designed to remedy the intensity of the evil of the fall by its religion, and the universality of the evil by its Church, has succeeded in the first, because its religion has been retained as God gave it, but has failed in the second, because its Church has been greatly corrupted.

Christianity, then, contains on the one hand a divine philosophy, which we may call its religion, and a divine polity, which is its Church.

But it is precisely from an acknowledgment of this last truth, accompanied with a misunderstanding of its real nature, that the greatest part of the actual mischief has arisen. When we say, therefore, that Christianity contains a divine polity, namely, its Church, it is of the utmost importance that we have a clear notion of the Christian Church, according to what we may gather from the Scripture to have been the mind of its Divine Founder.

Now, that religion should be a social as well as an individual concern, is nothing peculiar to Christianity, if by religion we mean the outward and visible worship of God. The act of sacrifice, almost of necessity, involves the co-operation of more than a single person;—festivals and solemn processions, even hymns of thanksgiving and praise, can scarcely be performed by one alone. Religion, then, in that sense in which the ancient world generally understood it, that is, public and visible worship, has always been, and must always be, the business of several persons together;—the religion of a single individual must, in this sense, be something imperfect, and only in a very small degree possible.

But the peculiarity of Christianity consists in this, that while it takes religion in another sense, and means by it, not the visible worship of God, but the service of the heart towards him; and whilst it would thus appear that religion could exist perfectly in one single individual, and required no co-operation of more persons, yet still it is made the business of a number or multitude, and our spiritual relations to God are represented as matters of a joint interest, no less than that visible worship which, in its very nature, must be more than individual.

Now, it is seen and generally acknowledged that men's physical welfare has been greatly promoted by the co-operation of a number of persons endowed with unlike powers and resources. One man having what another wants, and wanting what another has, there is an obvious wisdom in so combining their efforts, as that the strength of one should supply the weakness of another, and so the weakness should in no case be perceptible.

This co-operative principle, founded on the great dissimilarity which prevails amongst men, was by

Christianity to be applied to moral purposes, as it had long been to physical[a]; each man was to regard his intellectual and moral gifts as a means of advancing the intellectual and moral good of society; what he himself wanted was to be supplied out of the abundance of his neighbour;—and thus the moral no less than the physical weaknesses of each individual, were to be strengthened and remedied, till they should vanish as to their enfeebling effects both with respect to himself and to the community.

Nothing could be more general than such a system of co-operation. It extended to every part of life; not only going far beyond that co-operation for ritual purposes, which was the social part of the old religions, but, so far as men's physical well-being had been the sole object of existing civil societies, it went far beyond them also. For though it is possible, and unhappily too easy, to exclude moral considerations from our notions of physical good, and from our notions of ritual religion, yet it is not easy, in looking to the moral good of man, to exclude considerations of his physical well-being. Every outward thing having a tendency to affect his moral character, either for the better or for the worse, and this especially holding good with respect to riches or poverty,

[a] [See Introduction to Sermons on Christian Life, its Course, its Hindrances, and its Helps, p. xlviii.]

economical questions, in all their wide extent, fall directly under the cognizance of those whose object is to promote man's moral welfare.

But while thus general, the object of Christian co-operation was not to be vague. When men combined to offer sacrifice, or to keep festival, there was a definite object of their union; but the promotion of man's moral welfare might seem indistinct and lost in distance. Something nearer and more personal was therefore to be mixed up with that which was indistinct from its very vastness. The direct object of Christian co-operation was to bring Christ into every part of common life; in scriptural language, to make human society one living body, closely joined in communion with Christ, its Head. And for this purpose, one of the very simplest acts of natural necessity was connected with the very deepest things of religion; —the meal of an assembly of Christians was made the sacrament of the body and blood of Christ. And the early church well entered into the spirit of this ordinance, when it began every day by a partaking of the holy communion. For when Christ was thus brought into one of the commonest acts of nature and of common society, it was a lively lesson, that in every other act through the day he should be made present also: if Christians at their very social meal could enter into the highest spiritual communion, it taught them that in all matters of life, even when separated from one another bodily, that same communion should be preserved inviolate; that in all things they were working for and with one another, with and to Christ and God.

Such appears, even from the meagre account of a stranger, to have been the manner of living of the Christians of Bithynia, about a hundred years after the birth of our Lord, and about seventy therefore from the first preaching of Christianity. They met before day, and sang together a hymn to Christ: then they bound themselves to one another by oath,—according to Pliny's expression, " sacramento," but in reality, we may be sure, by their joint partaking of the communion of Christ's body and blood,—that they would neither steal, nor rob, nor commit adultery, nor break faith, nor refuse to restore what had been entrusted to them. Then they went to their day's work, and met again to partake their meal together; which they probably hallowed, either by making it a direct communion, or by some prayers, or hymns, which reminded them of their Christian fellowship.

Now in this account, short as it is, we see the two great principles of the Christian Church: first, co-operation for general moral improvement, for doing the duties of life better; and secondly, the bringing Christ as it were into their communion, by beginning the day with him, and deriving their principle of virtuous living directly from his sacrament. The Church of Bithynia existed on a small scale, in a remote province; but here are precisely those leading principles of the Christian Church exemplified, which were fitted for all circumstances and all places, and which contain in them that essential virtue which the Church was to embody and to diffuse.

It is obvious, also, that the object of Christian society being thus extensive, and relating not to ritual observances, but to the improvement of the whole of our life, the natural and fit state of the Church is, that it should be a sovereign society or commonwealth; as long as it is subordinate and municipal, it cannot fully carry its purposes into effect. This will be evident, if we consider that law and government are the sovereign influences on human society; that they in the last resort shape and control it at their pleasure; that institutions depend on them, and are by them formed and modified; that what they sanction will ever be generally considered innocent; that what they condemn is thereby made a crime, and if persisted in becomes rebellion; and that those who hold in their hands the power of life and death must be able greatly to obstruct the progress of whatever they disapprove of, and those who dispose of all the honours and rewards of society must, in the same way, be greatly able to advance whatever they think excellent. So long, then, as the sovereign society is not Christian, and the Church is not sovereign, we have two powers alike designed to act upon the whole of our being, but acting often in opposition to one another. Of these powers, the one has wisdom, the other external force and influence; and from the division of these things, which ought ever to go together, the wisdom of the Church cannot carry into effect the truths which it sees and loves; whilst the power of government, not being guided by wisdom, influences society for evil rather than for good [a].

The natural and true state of things then is, that this power and this wisdom should be united; that human life should not be pulled to pieces between two claimants, each pretending to exercise control over it, not in some particular portion, but universally; that wisdom should be armed with power, power guided by wisdom; that the Christian Church should have no external force to thwart its beneficent purposes; that government should not be poisoned by its internal ignorance or wickedness, and thus advance the cause of God's enemy, rather than perform the part of God's vicegerent.

This is the perfect notion of a Christian Church,

[a] [See Lectures on Modern History (Inaug. Lect. and Appendix).]

that it should be a sovereign society, operating therefore with full power for raising its condition, first morally, and then physically; operating through the fullest development of the varied faculties and qualities of its several members, and keeping up continually, as the bond of its union, the fellowship of all its people with one another through Christ, and their communion with him as their common Head.

With this notion of a perfect Church two things are utterly inconsistent:—first, the destroying of the principle of co-operation through the varied talents and habits of the several members of the society, and substituting in the place of it a system in which a very few should be active and the great mass passive[a]; a system in which vital heat was to be maintained, not by the even circulation of the blood through every limb, through the healthy co-operation of the arteries and veins of every part, but by external rubbing and chafing, when the limbs, from a suspension of their inward activity, had become cold and paralysed.

Secondly, the taking of any part or parts of human life out of its control, by a pretended distinction between spiritual things and secular—a distinction utterly without foundation: for in one sense all things are secular, for they are done in

[a] [Introd. to Sermons on Christian Life, its Course, its Hindrances, and its Helps, pp. xlviii. xlix.]

time and on earth; in another, all things are spiritual, for they affect us morally either for the better or the worse, and so tend to make our spirits fitter for the society of God or of his enemies. The division rests entirely on principles of heathenism, and tends to make Christianity, like the religions of the old world, not a sovereign discipline for every part and act of life, but a system for communicating certain abstract truths, and for the performance of certain visible rites and ceremonies.

These two notions, both utterly inconsistent with the idea of a true Christian Church, have been prevalent, alternately or conjointly, almost from the very beginning of Christianity. To the first we owe Popery in all its shapes, Romanist or Protestant; the second is the more open form of Antichrist, which, by its utter dissoluteness, has gone far to reduce countries nominally Christian to a state of lawlessness and want of principle worse than the worst heathenism.

But these two Antichrists have ever prepared the way for each other; and the falsehood of the one has led directly to the falsehood of its apparent opposite, but real ally and co-operator.

I begin, then, with the first of these two evils: the substitution of the activity of some in place of the activity of all; the distinction of the grand characteristic of the Christian Church, the co-operation, namely, of society through the several faculties and qualities of its members, for the attainment of the highest moral good of all.

This life, as it may well be called, of the Church, may be injured by an extreme predominance of the activity of some members, by which the others are necessarily rendered less active. A mere exaggeration of the principles of government may effect this, and it may arise out of the most benevolent feelings. Kind and earnest teachers commit this very mistake when they assist their pupil too much; they feel that they can do the work better than he can, and that their assistance will enable him to accomplish his task in a shorter time, and more effectually. But they really injure him; because the greater completeness and clearness of any one particular piece of knowledge is a far less benefit than the strengthening of his own faculties by exercise: the knowledge thus given is not power, but is gained at the cost of power, and is a hindrance rather than a help to the wholesome acquisition of knowledge hereafter. Even so benevolent governments, seeing the ignorance and mistaken notions of their people, are eager to fence them in on every side by their own care, and to act for them, because they were likely of themselves to act wrong. But, unhappily, with the tares they thus pluck up the good seed also; the people get accustomed to let the government act for them; they thus may acquire the innocence of infancy or death, but they acquire also the incapacity of those states for good; and the result is, not a living spirit, but a lifeless corpse.

Still, it must not be forgotten that with government the error is only in the excess or in the unseasonableness of its activity. In itself it is beneficent and necessary. Its abuses are no argument against its existence; it is founded on truth, and is indispensable in every state of society. But the life of the Church was impaired far more fatally by the introduction of another principle very distinct from that of government, the principle of priesthood. Persons unaccustomed to examine the subject thoroughly have often very confused ideas about priesthood; they profess utterly to disclaim it, while in fact they are zealously maintaining it. But the essential point in the notion of a priest is this, that he is a person made necessary to our intercourse with God, without being necessary or beneficial to us morally. His interference makes the worshipper neither a wiser man nor a holier than he would have been without it; and yet it is held to be indispensable. This unreasonable, immoral, unspiritual necessity is the essence of the idea of priesthood.

Priesthood, then, is properly mediation, taking

this last word in its etymological rather than in its common meaning. When the act on the worshipper's part is already complete, whether the worship be ritual or spiritual, the presence or interference of a priest is made a necessary medium through which alone the act can be presented to God. For instance, suppose that the worshipper has a right belief concerning God, and knows what he desires to ask of God, the act of prayer on his part is complete; but if it be said that his prayer must be offered to God by another, and that otherwise God will not accept it, then here is the exact notion of priesthood. It ceases to be priesthood, and becomes teaching or assistance, if the act on the worshipper's part cannot be morally or reasonably complete without the aid of another. He who knows not what to pray for, cannot by himself complete the act of prayer, but requires to be taught in order to do it. This teaching, however, is not priesthood, because the necessity for its interposition is reasonable, moral, and spiritual.

A priest, therefore, as he does not make the worshipper more fit to worship in himself, implies necessarily that man cannot approach God. The necessity for his mediation arises out of this: man cannot approach God, but he may approach to some other being, and this other being may approach God. Thus this intermediate being stands to man in the place of God, and man's direct relations towards God himself are declared to be an impossibility.

We have arrived at a great and divine truth; the very foundation stone, indeed, of Christianity. We cannot come to God directly; we require one to be to us in the place of God. But one in the place of God and not God, is as it were a falsehood; it is the mother falsehood from which all idolatry is derived. The mystery of Christianity has met this necessity of our nature, and at the same time has avoided the evil of the falsehood. We have one who is to us in the place of God, but who is also God truly;—we have one whom we may approach, although we cannot approach God, for he is also truly man.

It has been well said, that no error is mere error; something there is of truth ever mixed with it. So the error of human priesthoods does indeed but express a great truth, that man cannot come to God without a mediator. But this truth is to man, when left to his own devices, either useless or mischievous. He attempts to act upon it by devising for himself a human mediator, and he falls at once into superstition and idolatry.

Again, the human mediator, as I have said before, does nothing to bring us in ourselves really nearer to God. His interference at all, implies that we are separated from God; this separation

[c]

is a moral thing, arising out of our unlikeness to God. But the human mediator does nothing to restore to us God's likeness. It is strictly true, therefore, that his interposition has no moral value; it makes us neither better nor holier; it therefore shows the falsehood of its own claim; for while professing to bring us to God, it leaves us as far from him as ever.

But the true Mediator does not so: while he reconciles God to man, he also reconciles man to God. He works by his Spirit upon our own nature, and weeds out from it the seeds as it were of our alienation from God. Thus he does bring us near to God, for he makes us like God. And he is our one and only Priest, our one and only Mediator.

Some there are who profess to join cordially in this doctrine, and ask who disputes it. So little do they understand the very tenets which they uphold. For they themselves dispute and deny it, inasmuch as they maintain that the sacraments are necessary to salvation, and that they can only be effectually administered by a man appointed after a certain form. And thus they set up again the human mediator, which is idolatry, and they show the falsehood of his claim, because they make a man like ourselves necessary to bring us near to God; and this man, who is to complete Christ's work, and reconcile to God those whom

Christ had left alienated, cannot touch the slightest part of the soul or mind of any one. If we were separated from God, he cannot bring us to him; for we remain in ourselves, when his ministration is over, just the same as we were before.

This dogma, then, of a human priesthood in Christ's church, appointed to administer his sacraments, and thereby to mediate between God and man, from no reasonable or moral necessity, is a thing quite distinct from any exaggerated notions of the activity of government: it is not the excess of a beneficent truth, but it is, from first to last, considering that it is addressed to Christians, who have their Divine Priest and Mediator already, a mere error; and an error not merely speculative, but fraught with all manner of mischief, idolatrous and demoralizing, destructive of Christ's Church; injurious to Christ and to his Spirit; the worst and earliest form of Antichrist.

This error is demoralizing, because it has led to the false distinction between secular things and spiritual, and has tended to bring back Christianity to the likeness of a heathen religion, by changing it from a law of life to a matter of rites and outward observances; from which the care of the general moral character of every man is a thing altogether different.

It has led to the false distinction between secular things and spiritual. For in all the acts of life into which it was the design of Christianity to bring God and Christ, the priest is altogether excluded. In the works of justice and mercy, in the feelings of devotion, of hope, of fear, of love, the priest can find no place, for what is real and moral repels him. His element is only what is formal, shadowy, ceremonial; and in order to make himself of importance, he must raise what is shadowy and ceremonial into the place of what is real and moral. Men can act in life without him, and feel without him; but he tells them that certain ceremonial acts cannot be performed without him, and then he goes on and teaches that these ceremonial acts are the essence of religion.

But in Christianity his task was hard, because even in its very ceremonies the essence was something real and moral. When Christians met together and received the bread and wine of their common living as the body and blood of Christ, such an act had a real tendency to strengthen and confirm their souls, and the Holy Spirit made such a communion a constant means of grace to those who partook of it. But here there was no placef or the priest; on the one side there was Christ's Church assembled, on the other there was Christ and his Spirit to bless them. The priest then steps in, diverts attention from the moral part of this communion, from its peculiar union of things divine and human, of social feelings and religious, from its hallowing of common life, by making us even eat and drink to God's glory and our own salvation, and fixes it upon a supposed mystical virtue conveyed to the bread and wine by the pronouncing of certain words over them by a certain person. The bread and wine became the sacrament of Christ's body and blood according to Christ's ordinance, by the assembled church receiving them as such; by their converting an act of nature into an act of religion; by their agreeing to partake together as of their earthly food, so also of their spiritual, and thus being joined to one another in Christ. The agreement, therefore, of those communicating, their common faith and love, constitute the real consecration of the bread and wine; it is this which, through Christ's Spirit, changes the supper into the sacrament.

But the priest says, "Not so: it is not your common faith and purpose to celebrate the communion; it is not the fact of Christ having died and risen again which can bring him to you or you to him: I must interpose, and pronounce certain words over the bread and over the cup; and then what neither your faith nor Christ's redemption of you had made other than common food, becomes now, through my mediation, a thing endowed with a divine virtue; nay, it is become Christ himself.

Whether there be any communion of yourselves or no, whether you are alone or with one another, whether you are concurring in spirit or no, still because I, the priest, have pronounced certain words over it, it has acquired a miraculous power, and unless you are partakers of this you cannot be saved." So the communion of the Church, which morally was so essential, is thus made unessential; and the uttering certain words by a particular person, of which neither Christ nor his apostles had said any thing, and which morally can have no virtue at all, is made essential. And thus was the Church supplanted by the priest; and the communion, which is the very life of the Church, became the mass, with all its superstitions and idolatries.

The Church being set aside, and the principal part in the communion being transferred from it to the priest, his office grew in importance, and the Church, in the same proportion, became removed from Christ, and desecrated. Then the priest was regarded as the minister of Christ in spiritual things, the Church only in temporal. For not only in the communion, but in the public prayers and exhortations of the Church, the Church itself was reduced more and more to a passive condition,—the priest alone was active. Thus there were some whose business was religion, and others whose business it was not. Religion and life were separated; the one was called spiritual, when it was in reality become less so; the other was called, and became too truly, secular. The salt which Christ had given to the Church, that each man might by it render the world and worldly things pure and holy to him, the Church had now to seek from the priest; and because it was to be sought from another, it in great measure lost its savour.

CHAPTER II.

It has been stated generally that the efficacy of the Church has been destroyed by the excess of a good and necessary principle, that of government, and the introduction of another principle wholly false and mischievous, that of priesthood. The first in itself the Church recognises, and must ever recognise; the second she wholly repudiates. And thus we shall find that, while there is much said in Scripture in commendation of the one, the other is altogether omitted, as an element belonging to Heathenism and not to Christianity.

Now, omitting all the commandments given us to obey government in general, and all such passages as claim obedience to the Apostles personally, we find several injunctions to submit ourselves to the rulers of the Church, being Christians, and yet not being Apostles;—and all these injunctions are a proof of our first position, that the principle of government in the Christian Church is recognised and sanctioned in the Scriptures.

I. St. Paul, in the earliest of all his Epistles,

the first to the Thessalonians, entreats the church of Thessalonica to acknowledge or recognise, εἰ-δέναι, those that laboured among them, and were over them in the Lord, and who admonished them, νουθετοῦντας ὑμας. And he calls on the church to "esteem them very highly in love for their work's sake."[a]

II. In two passages, (Galatians vi. 6, and 1 Timothy v. 17,) he asserts the claim of the governors of the church to be maintained by the church. In the first, indeed, he speaks only of such governors of the church as are instructors; κοινωνείτω δὲ ὁ κατηχούμενος τὸν λόγον τῷ κατηχοῦντι, ἐν πᾶσιν ἀγαθοῖς;—but in the second passage, while he acknowledges the especial claim of such, he extends the right to all rulers of the church generally, whatever may be their particular functions : οἱ καλῶς προεστῶτες πρεσβύτεροι διπλῆς τιμῆς ἀξιούσθωσαν.

III. The writer of the Epistle to the Hebrews says also, " Obey your rulers, and submit to them ; "—and that this means the Christian rulers of the church is evident by what follows, " for they watch as men who are to give an account for your souls ; "—which of course could not be said of Heathen authorities.

IV. To these may be added all that is said of the qualifications of an ἐπίσκοπος in the first

[a] 1 Tuess. v. 12, 13.

Epistle to Timothy and in that to Titus; and which implies that government in the church was a thing essential, and recognised from the beginning.

V. St. Peter, as if writing under the liveliest recollection of our Lord's charge to himself, and of the strong contrast which Christ had drawn between the common practice of heathen government and that which should prevail among Christians, thus writes in his first Epistle (v. 2) to the elders of the several churches—" Feed the flock of God which is among you, taking the oversight thereof" (ἐπισκοποῦντες), " not by constraint, but willingly;" (Lachmann adds κατὰ θεόν, 'as becomes a servant and child of God;') " not for filthy lucre," (which implies that lucre *might* be a motive, that is, that the rulers of the church were maintained by the church,) " but of a ready mind."

VI. We read also in the Acts, that Paul and Barnabas appointed elders to govern the churches which they founded in Lycaonia and the south of Asia Minor[a]; and St. Paul addresses the elders of the church of Ephesus[b], in the same language as St. Peter, charging them "to feed the church of God." Now this term of "feeding as a shepherd feeds his flock," is one of the oldest and most universal metaphors to express a supreme and at the same time a beneficent government.

It is needless to multiply other passages, as

[a] xiv. 23.   [b] xx. 28.

those already quoted are abundantly sufficient to show that Christianity supposes and sanctions the principle of government in the church, and reciprocally the principle of obedience; that in this respect the church was to resemble all other societies;—some of its members were to rule and others were to be subject.

But of the principle of priesthood, by which one man or set of men are declared to be necessary mediators for their brethren, so that without them their brethren cannot worship God acceptably or be suffered to approach him, the Scriptures contain not one word, except as rejecting and condemning it. This of course cannot be shown by extracts as to the negative part of it: it will be sufficient to show that the passages usually quoted by the advocates of the priesthood as sanctioning their notions are all misinterpreted, or misapplied; and then to give some passages which assert the contrary to the doctrine of the priesthood, and describe it as one of the great privileges of the Christian Church, that its one great High Priest Jesus Christ has given it full access to God for ever, so that there is nothing for priesthood to do, or rather for human priesthood to pretend to do for it, any more, so long as earth shall endure.

The principle of priesthood unmixed with any other is seen in the Christian Church most plainly in the claim to administer the Lord's Supper. I say this rather than, in the claim to administer the sacraments generally, or in the so-called power of the keys,—because although something of the notion of priesthood has undoubtedly been mixed with both these, and especially with the latter; and although in practice absolution has come to be a proper priestly act, yet in their origin both the power of baptizing and that of absolving were in a great degree acts of government; being in fact the power of admitting or of restoring members to the privileges of the Christian society. But the claim of administering the Lord's Supper is the assumption of a power exclusively priestly; it interposes in an act with which government has nothing to do, and its supposed object is merely inward and spiritual—to give a spiritual efficacy to that which without its interference would have been common food. The Scripture, then, might recognise an exclusive power of baptizing or of excommunicating and absolving, without at all countenancing the notion of a priesthood, because it might view such a power as one naturally belonging to the rulers of any society, and as connected therefore with government only. But if it be found to recognise an exclusive claim of administering the Lord's Supper, then no doubt it must be allowed in the strictest sense to recognise in Christianity a human priesthood.

THE CHURCH. 29

This power is said accordingly to be recognised by the Apostle Paul in two passages, 1 Corinth. iv. 1, and again in the same Epistle, x. 16.

I. In the first passage St. Paul says, "Let a man so account of us as of the ministers of Christ, and *stewards of the mysteries of God.*" It is contended that, by this last expression, St. Paul means to say that himself and his fellow ministers were "dispensers of the sacraments."

But, in the first place, Baptism and the Lord's Supper are not in the Scripture sense mysteries at all. A mystery, in the Scripture, is a hidden truth;—almost always, it signifies a truth hidden generally from men, but revealed to the people of God. By a figure, Christ himself is twice called "the mystery of God," or "of godliness,"[a] because his manifestation in the flesh is the great truth which Christianity has revealed to us. Baptism and the Lord's Supper are actions connected with the Christian mysteries, but they are not mysteries themselves; much less are they so especially deserving of the term as to engross it to themselves, and to become the prominent idea expressed by it.

Again; by whatever name St. Paul might have called himself, it certainly would not have been "a dispenser of the sacraments." He had just before said that his business was not to baptize,

[a] Coloss. i. 27. 1 Tim. iii. 16.

but to preach the gospel; that, so far from its being his office to "dispense the sacraments," he had only baptized three or four individuals in the course of his whole ministry at Corinth. He who thus studiously devolved on others the ministration of one of the sacraments, could scarcely have desired the Corinthians to regard him as being appointed especially to dispense them.

On the other hand, we find him saying, a little before, that he and his fellow ministers were in the habit of speaking of "the wisdom of God in a mystery," or rather " God's secret or hidden wisdom,"—the wisdom hidden from men, which God foreordained before the world unto our glory. And again, further on in the Epistle, he uses the expression, "I have had a dispensation" (or 'stewardship,' if οἰκόνομος in the former passage be translated 'steward') "entrusted to me." Now this dispensation is so certainly the "dispensation of the Gospel," by preaching, that the gloss εὐαγγελίου has actually found its way into the text, and is expressed in the common editions, and in our translation. It is shown by the whole context, in which he repeatedly says that his business is "to preach the gospel." There can be no doubt, therefore, that when he describes himself as "a steward or dispenser of the mysteries of God," he means that very same "speaking of the wisdom of God in a mystery," that very same " dispensation of the Gospel by preaching," which in other parts of this Epistle he declares to have been his business as an Apostle; just as he declares also that "to dispense the sacraments" was not his business; for he says, "God called me not to baptize, but to preach the Gospel."

II. The second passage is as follows: "The cup of blessing which we bless, is it not a communion of the blood of Christ? The bread which we break, is it not a communion of the body of Christ?" This shows, it is argued, that it belonged to the Apostles to bless the cup at the communion, and to break the bread; in other words, to consecrate the elements, and so to give to them their sacramental character and virtue. It is necessary to say that I have myself heard and read this interpretation; I do not pretend to know how many there are who adopt it.

It is evident that the whole force of this passage depends on the meaning of the word "we." If "we" means "we Apostles," as distinguished from other Christians, then the argument would have some plausibility; but if "we" means not "we Apostles," but "we Christians," then the whole argument falls to the ground at once. Now the very next verse goes on as follows: "For we being many are one bread and one body, for we are all partakers of that one bread." It is then, not "we the Apostles," but "we Christians," "we being many," "we all," "who bless the cup of blessing, and break the bread." So far from proving that there exists in Christianity a priestly power in the administration of the communion, this passage rather shows the contrary.

The contrary also fully appears from the general language of the New Testament. It is declared as plainly as words can speak, that, in a religious sense, all Christians are equal before God, and that all are brought near to him, have access to him, are reconciled to him, are his heirs and his children. Now some of these terms were applicable to the whole Jewish church, and yet in that church there was undoubtedly a human priesthood. But the Epistle to the Hebrews shows the great distinction, when it says that "we are sanctified by the offering of the body of Jesus Christ once for all;" that sacrifices must therefore cease to be offered; and that as the especial object of the Jewish priesthood was to sacrifice, so it may be presumed, that where no sacrifice remains to be offered[a], so neither should there be any priest. It is not pretended that all Christians are equal socially; for some are governors, and others are governed: nor are they so equal as to render distinctions for order's sake in their public meetings

---

[a] For his own view of what was the true Christian sacrifice still continued, see Introd. to Serm. vol. iv. p. 1; Serm. vol. v. p. 273.

unnecessary; for women are not allowed to speak in the congregation: but they are equal religiously, as being all alike redeemed by Christ, and brought by him near to God; that is, put into a condition to offer to him acceptably all religious offices; and in the only remaining kind of sacrifice, the spiritual offering of themselves to God, commanded to be, every man his own priest; inasmuch as by ourselves alone can our own hearts and bodies be devoted as thank-offerings to him who made them and redeemed them.

We find, then, no place in Scripture for the notion that any human mediation is required in order to perfect the purely religious acts of Christians. As all Christians can pray acceptably through Christ's mediation, so can all communicate acceptably in the signs of his body and blood;—such communion being manifestly not an act peculiar to the rulers of the society, but belonging to all the members of it, and therein differing from baptism, which is an act of government, so to speak, as well as an act of religion; and may, therefore, be fitly appropriated to one particular order of society, not as priests, but as governors.

It will be understood in what sense I call baptism an act of government, if it be considered that it is, amongst other things, the admission of a new member into the Christian society, and that, as such, it belongs properly to those who have authority given to them in that society; for where is the private individual, who is allowed at his own choice to admit strangers to the rights of citizenship in the commonwealth? It does not follow that baptism is nothing more than an act of government; but because it is clearly this, whatever it may be besides, therefore it is at least possible that when the power of administering it is ascribed exclusively to one particular order in the Church, there should be in this no allowance of any priestly power, but simply of the power of the magistrates or rulers of a society. We shall see, by-and-by, that this distinction is not unimportant.

Farther: it may appear on examination, that the very power of the keys itself, when rightly understood, implies nothing of a priesthood, but only the legitimate power of government.

It will be asked, however, what is the right understanding of this well-known expression, "The power of the keys"? And the answer must not be given lightly; for we are here concerned not with the careless words of fallible men, but with a solemn promise to the Church, made at three several times by Christ our Lord. Undoubtedly, therefore, the power of the keys means something, and that meaning cannot be a matter of indifference.

The promise was made by our Lord on three several occasions, viz. :—

1st. To St. Peter, apparently as a reward to that Apostle for his confessing his Master to be the Christ [a].

2nd. To the whole body or church of Christians, as a sanction to their sentence, when he had ordered that all quarrels between Christian and Christian should in the last resort be referred to the decision of the Church [b].

3rd. To the eleven Apostles, when our Lord, after his resurrection, was giving them their commission to found and govern his Church [c].

In the first two of these promises the words are identical, and they are figurative. They run, " Whatsoever thou " (or ' ye ') " shalt bind on earth shall be bound in heaven: and whatsoever thou " (or 'ye') " shalt loose on earth shall be loosed in heaven." In the third the words are different, although the sense is generally supposed to be nearly the same. They are, " Whosesoever sins ye remit, they are remitted unto them; and whosesoever sins ye retain, they are retained."

"To bind and to loose" are metaphors certainly, but metaphors easily to be understood. They express a legislative and a judicial power. To bind, legislatively, is to impose a general obligation—to say that a thing ought to be done or ought not to be done—to bind men's consciences either to the

---

[a] St. Matthew, xvi. 19.   [b] St. Matthew, xviii. 18.
St. John, xx. 23.

doing of it, or to the abstaining from it. Thus, St. Paul speaks of a woman being bound so long as her husband lives; but of being free to marry whom she will, if her husband be dead. In the one case there was a binding of the conscience, in the other a loosing of it. And this is one part of the sense of the expression. Again: to bind judicially, is to impose a particular obligation on an individual, to oblige him to do or to suffer certain things for the sake of justice, which, if left to himself, he would not choose to do or suffer. And to loose judicially, is to pronounce a man free from any such obligation; to declare that justice does not require of him, in this particular case, to do or to suffer anything for its satisfaction. Justice has no claim upon him—she leaves him free. This is the second part of the expression.

It is to this second part, to the binding and loosing judicially, that the third promise of our Lord belongs. For the retaining and remitting of sins is clearly a judicial power: the retaining of sin is the pronouncing that a man is bound to do or suffer something as a satisfaction for it; the remitting of sin is the pronouncing that justice has no hold upon him—that he is acquitted, loosed, freed from all her demands on him.

But such a legislative and judicial power is a power of government;—government, in fact, consisting mainly of these two great powers, the legislative and judicial. We do not as yet find anything, then, in the power of the keys that bears any relation to priesthood, according to that definition of it which was given above—that it is an interposition between God and man supposed to be necessary to our acceptance with God, yet without being necessary or beneficial to us morally. And this is strictly the idea of priestly absolution. For whether it be said that he who is absolved is forgiven by God, or that he who is not absolved is not forgiven by God, there is in either case an act made essential or beneficial to our salvation, which yet makes us morally neither the better nor the worse. Absolution, then, so understood, is a proper act of priesthood. But does such a power of absolution form any part of the Christian power of the keys?

It has been contended that it does, and our Lord's words to his Apostles are appealed to as the proof of this:—" Whosoever sins ye remit, they are remitted unto them; and whosoever sins ye retain, they are retained." Now, here there are two questions:—First, What was the meaning of our Lord's promise as addressed to the Apostles? Secondly, How much of this meaning was intended to apply to any except the Apostles?

1st. It is allowed that this promise conferred on the Apostles a judicial power, as distinct from a legislative one; it gave them authority to decide on individual cases; to pronounce that such or such a man was forgiven, in some sense or other, and that such or such a man was not forgiven. But the great question is, whether this power can be shown to be distinct from a power of government—that is, were the forgiveness or refusal of forgiveness here spoken of distinct from some outward sentence passed upon a man with reference to the Christian society; and were they grounded upon any thing more than actions cognizable by human perception, and therefore the fit objects of human reward or censure? For the peculiarity of a priestly power consists in this: that its sentence, in its essence, is not outward but inward; affecting a man not in his relations to the Christian society, but in his relations towards God, and grounded therefore upon a knowledge of more than actions cognizable by human perception—namely, of the thoughts and motives of the heart. For there is no doubt that our state towards God depends mainly on the state of our hearts, so that a judgment of the former cannot be passed without a knowledge of the latter.

We must separate, then, all such judicial acts as the declaration of forgiveness implied in the admission of new converts to baptism; and as the declaration of the retaining of sins implied in the striking of Elymas with blindness, in the visiting the incestuous Corinthian with some bodily punishment, in excommunication, and in the deaths of Ananias and Sapphira. In all these cases there was an outward sentence, affecting men outwardly and visibly in their earthly condition, and this sentence was grounded on some outward action;—in baptism, for instance, on the *profession* of repentance and faith, and in the other instances on acts of a similar character to those which human law habitually punishes.

But can we find, over and above such instances as these, any cases in which the Apostles, without any visible or outward sentence, passed a judgment simply on the state of an individual towards God; and a judgment founded, not on outward and tangible acts, but on a knowledge of the sincerity or insincerity of his feelings? We read of no such cases; but we find such language used respecting Christ's judgment, and God's knowledge of the thoughts of the heart, as is agreeable to our common impression, that of the state of a man's heart with respect to God, God is the only judge[a].

It may seem that in one instance an Apostle did possess a power of reading the heart, when Paul is said to have perceived that the cripple, who stedfastly listened to his speech at Lystra,

[a] [1 Sam. xvi. 7. 1 Kings viii. 39. Jerem. xvii. 9, 10. St. Luke xvi. 15. 1 Cor. iv. 4, 5.]

"had faith to be healed." It is not certain, however, that there was in this case any reading of the heart: " the stedfast listening," the expression of deep interest in Paul's words manifested in the whole countenance and attitude of the hearer, were an evidence not to be mistaken that he was thoroughly convinced by what he heard. But admitting for a moment that the Apostle's was a deeper judgment than he could have formed by his mere natural faculties, yet in this case we have God's warrant that he had judged rightly, inasmuch as the man's faith was proved by his being cured of his lameness at Paul's word. So that, even if there was a sentence grounded on such things as man cannot naturally discern, yet the proof was given that the judgment was right, by its being followed by an outward consequence greater than man alone could have effected.

2nd. So much of the power given by our Lord to his Apostles, as depended on their possessing a greater than human knowledge, would not, of course, be given to those who do not possess that knowledge. And if any man says that he does possess such knowledge, and if the claim does not prove itself, as in prophecy or in telling to a man what was in his thoughts, then we may call upon him for some sign that he does possess it. If he says positively that such a man has his sins forgiven in the sight of God, then he should tell him, as St. Paul did, to stand upright on his feet, or should relieve him from some trouble or infirmity by which he is manifestly afflicted. If he says as positively that such and such a man is not forgiven, then let him also show his power of delivering such an one to Satan for the destruction of the flesh, that his spirit might be saved in the day of the Lord.

It does not appear that the Apostles ever exercised what was, properly, a priestly power. Admitting however, for the moment, that they had exercised it, yet as such a power is of an extraordinary character, and requires more than the ordinary attributes of human nature to exercise it properly, and as the Apostles were endowed with certain extraordinary gifts, such as are not possessed by men in general, we should be justified in assuming some connexion between their power and their gifts, and might safely conclude that those who had not the latter could not enjoy the former. But the case is stronger, now that it cannot be shown that even the Apostles possessed a priestly power. If such a power was too great even for them to wield, how can it be supposed that others could wield it, on whom none of their extraordinary qualifications have descended?

The nearest approach to a priestly power recognised in the New Testament is in the effects of intercessory prayer; for if we pray for grace for our brother, and God grants our prayer, we seem to be in some sort the channel of God's mercy to him, without producing any effect upon him morally; and this was laid down to be the characteristic of a priestly power, as distinct from a ministry or cure of souls, which acts on those committed to its charge through moral means.

First, however, the virtue of intercessory prayer is, in itself, widely different from the pretended priestly power to give a virtue to the sacraments. The peculiarly unchristian part of this latter claim is this, that it makes a human mediator necessary to those who are actually acknowledging, trusting in, and earnestly desiring to enjoy the fruits of, Christ's mediation; whereas no one would say that our own prayers, offered up according to Christ's Spirit, and in Christ's name, will not be accepted, unless others will also pray for us. The prayers of others in our behalf are not made the condition on which alone our own earnest prayers shall be accepted.

Intercessory prayer in its highest cases supposes that a man has not the grace of repentance and faith—that he is not at present morally in a state of acceptance with God. It is the very worst part of his condition, that he will not pray for himself. Under these circumstances, that God should have graciously left a way open by which his friends may labour with hope in his behalf; that over and above the secret and inscrutable ways by which he, according to his own pleasure, sometimes touches the heart of the impenitent sinner, he should have also revealed one way in which the love of his friends may work for him—this would be a very different thing from declaring that a man's own faith, and love, and prayers, shall be of no use unless other men shall also interpose for him. It is one thing to enable human charity to be serviceable to him who, if left to himself, would be lost, and another to allow human presumption to declare its aid necessary to him who, having received Christ's grace through faith, is already saved.

But there is yet another great difference which effectually separates the intercessory prayer of Christians from the mediation of a priesthood— namely, that its efficacy is not limited, or given especially, to the prayers of any one order of men: it is not the priest who is to pray for the people, but the ministers and the people who are to pray for each other—nay, a peculiar stress is laid on the efficacy of the united prayers of many; so that we may assume that the prayers of the people are at least as important to the minister, as his prayers are to them.

Here, however, we shall be referred to that well-known passage in the Epistle of St. James, which directs the sick to call in the elders of the

Church, and speaks of the elders praying over them and anointing them with oil in the name of the Lord, and of their being raised up by virtue of this prayer. Now here again a manifest distinction must be taken, between those elders who possessed the gift of healing, and others who have it not: it cannot be maintained that with regard to the especial subject there spoken of, the recovery, namely, of a sick person, a general conclusion follows as to the peculiar efficacy of the prayers of presbyters in all times, because they were peculiarly efficacious when combined with the gift of healing. But I should be unwilling to limit the words of the Apostle entirely to bodily cures, or to the circumstances of the early church. I would allow most readily, that they are of general and perpetual application, but their meaning makes against any priestly power in the clergy, rather than establishes it.

The object of the passage is to encourage the exercise of those mutual spiritual aids rendered by Christians to each other, which are one of the great objects and privileges of the institution of the Church. The body was to sympathize with its several members. If a man was in trouble, he was to pray; if in joy, to sing hymns: in neither case is the Apostle speaking of private prayer or private singing, but of those of the Christian congregation: there every individual Christian could find the best relief for his sorrows, and the liveliest sympathy in his joy. St. Paul's command, "Rejoice with them that do rejoice, and weep with them that weep," applies to this same sympathy, which the prayers and hymns of the Church Services were a constant means of expressing. But if a man were sick and could not go to the congregation, still he was not to lose the benefit of his Christian communion with them—he might then ask them to come to him; and as the whole congregation could not thus be summoned, the elders were to go as its representatives, and their prayers were to take the place of the prayers of the whole Church. Care, however, is taken to show that the virtue of their prayers arises not from their being priests, but from their being Christians, and standing in the place of the whole Church. For these words immediately follow: "Confess therefore to one another your sins, and pray for one another, that ye may be healed; there is much virtue in a just man's prayer, when it is offered earnestly." Now this most divine system of a living church, in which all were to aid each other, in which each man might open his heart to his neighbour, and receive the help of his prayers, and in which each man's earnest prayer, offered in Christ's name, had so high a promise of blessing annexed to it, has been most destroyed by that notion of a priesthood, which—claiming that men should confess their sins to the clergy, not as to their brethren, but as to God's vicegerents, and confining the promised blessing to the prayers of the clergy as priests, not as Christians, nor as the representatives of the whole Church—has changed the sympathy of a Christian society into the dominion of a priesthood, and the mingled carelessness and superstition of a laity.

St. John's language agrees with that of St. James: "If any man see his brother sinning a sin which is not unto death, he shall pray, and Christ shall give him life, for those who are not sinning unto death. There is a sin unto death;— it is not for that that I am bidding him to pray." Here the very same blessing which St. James speaks of as following the elder's prayers, is said by St. John to follow the prayer of any Christian; —a clear proof that the elders were sent for as the representatives of the Church, and not as if their prayers possessed a peculiar virtue, because they stood as priests between God and the people.

Thus, then, we find much in Scripture which recognises high powers of government in the Christian Church, but nothing which acknowledges a priesthood. The distinction is of immense importance, for from the covert intermixture of priesthood with government has followed the great corruption of the Divine plan of the Christian Church.

CHAPTER III.

THE chapter which I am now going to write is in truth superfluous. Nay, although its particular object were proved ever so fully, yet this would be a less gain than loss if any were, by the nature of the argument, encouraged to believe that we are to seek for our knowledge of Christianity anywhere else but in the Scriptures. What we find there is a part of Christianity, whether recognised as such or no in after ages; what we do not find there is no part of Christianity, however early or however general may have been the attempts to interpolate it. If this be not so, we must change our religion and our Master: we can be no longer Christians, servants of Christ, instructed by him and his own Apostles, but Alexandrianists, Syrianists, Asianists;—following the notions which happened to prevail in the Church according to the preponderance of particular local or temporary influences, and following as our master neither the wisdom of God, nor even the wisdom of men, but the opinions of a time and state of society, whose inferiority in all other respects is acknowledged,—and the guidance of individuals, not one of whom approaches nearly to that greatness which in the case of the great Greek philosophers made an implicit veneration for their decisions in some degree excusable.

If it could be shown that the unanimous voice of men eminent alike for goodness and for wisdom, had from the earliest times insisted upon some doctrine or practice not taught or commanded in the New Testament as an essential part of Christianity; if it should appear that this doctrine or practice were in no way favourable to their own importance or interest; and if it could be shown, also, that it was not in accordance with the way of thinking prevalent in their age and country,— but could have commended itself to their minds by nothing but its intrinsic excellence,—then, indeed, the doctrine might be concluded to be reasonable, and the practice good: but the omission of all notice of them by our Lord and his Apostles would be a fact so unaccountable and so staggering, that the triumph of ecclesiastical tradition would be the destruction of all well-grounded faith in the authenticity of our records of Christianity—nay, it would involve in the most painful uncertainty the very truth of the Christian revelation. For if Christ and his Apostles omitted any essential part of Christianity; if their revelation was not perfect; then the dispensation of the fulness of times must be sought for elsewhere: and the claim of Mohammedanism, that it is the perfecting of the earlier dispensations, the Jewish and Christian, ceases to be blasphemous. Or if it be said that the doctrine or practice in question were inculcated by Christ and his Apostles, although they are not noticed in the New Testament, then what is our security that other vital points have not been omitted in like manner in our epistles and gospels? And when we consider what the New Testament is; that it contains four detailed accounts of our Lord's life and teaching, one of which was written by his beloved disciple St. John; that it contains an account of the first propagation of Christianity by our Lord's Apostles; that it contains, farther, thirteen or fourteen epistles of St. Paul, written some to Churches, some to individuals, and comprehending systematic views of what Christianity is; appeals innumerable to its motives, its hopes, and its consolations; exhortations innumerable to cling to its truths and to walk in its precepts, with specific mention of these truths and precepts;—when we consider, farther, that we have in the same Scriptures an epistle from St. James, the head of the Church of Jerusalem, whose mind and views, humanly speaking, were least like those of St. Paul; and that we have epistles also from St. Peter and St. John,

[E]

two of our Lord's very chiefest Apostles, and that these epistles are addressed to Christians generally, and dwell on those points of Christian faith and life which it was most essential to bear in mind; then if all these writers, all these great Apostles, in these long and varied writings, have omitted with one accord themselves, and have represented our Lord as omitting, any essential doctrine or practice of Christianity, how can we believe that they were indeed partakers of that Holy Spirit which was to guide them into all truth? How can we think that they were really empowered by God to be the preachers and authoritative teachers of his revelation?

Or, thirdly, it may be said that the New Testament refers only to the beginnings of the Gospel; that the new converts received, indeed, τὰ ἀναγκαιότατα τῆς παιδείας τοῦ Χριστοῦ,—such truths as were most indispensable, and without which they could not have been Christians at all; but that the full development of the system of Christianity was reserved for a later season; that the Scriptures themselves imply this, inasmuch as, in the epistle to the Hebrews, a distinction is expressly drawn between the first principles of the doctrine of Christ and the going on unto perfection, and the writer of that epistle complains that they whom he was addressing were not yet fit for this more perfect truth. That in this manner the doctrine of the Christian priesthood and of the mystic virtue of the sacraments is not, indeed, fully developed in the New Testament, but was taught by the Apostles at the very close of their career, and received by the Church as their last and most perfect instruction, which was to complete the revelation of Christianity.

It has pleased God that of the peculiar teaching of the great majority of the Apostles we should know nothing; we cannot say with certainty what they taught individually at any period of their lives. But we can say positively that the latest teaching of St. Paul, St. Peter, and St. John contained in it no more perfect revelation concerning the priesthood and the sacraments than they had made known at the beginning of the gospel. St. Paul's second epistle to Timothy must surely be considered as containing his latest views of Christianity; and as being addressed to one who was himself a teacher, it must have contained those views fully; it cannot be pretended that St. Paul had any doctrine too esoterical to be communicated to Timothy. But his latest epistle, amidst many differences of expression from his earlier writings, such as the lapse of years brings to all men, contains in substance the very same view of Christianity which we find in the epistles to the Thessalonians. Paul's gospel is still Christ's resurrection, God's free salvation, Christ's coming to judgment. He is still as averse as ever to strifes about words; he warns Timothy that the time will come when Christians shall turn away their ears from the truth, and shall be turned unto fables. He refers him to his past doctrine ever since Timothy first knew him, not as to an imperfect system, to which he was now going to add some great truth hitherto suppressed, but as that very system which he earnestly wished to save from corruption and interpolation. This was Paul's language at a period when he declares that he had finished his course on earth, and had only to enter into his reward.

As we learn St. Paul's latest sentiments from his second epistle to Timothy, so we learn those of St. Peter from his second epistle general. He too speaks of himself in that epistle as leaving to the Church his dying admonition, as telling them the things which they might have always in remembrance after he was gone. Does this epistle contain that great doctrine of the priesthood and sacraments, which when he wrote his first epistle the Church was too weak to bear? In that first epistle, having used the expression "that baptism saved Christians," he hastens at once to explain his meaning, lest any should understand him superstitiously; and says that he does not mean by baptism's saving us, that the bodily washing with water saves, but the answer of a good conscience towards God, when men in repentance and faith were admitted into the fellowship of Christ's redemption. His explanation is clearly intended to draw off our attention from the outward rite to the moral state of the person receiving it: it was the repentance and faith of the person baptized, which, through God's mercy in Christ, saved him; and not the outward rite of immersion in water. Now, nothing is to be found in the second epistle which in any degree qualifies this: every word of his latest charge turns upon moral points; upon growth in all Christian graces, on improving to the utmost their knowledge of Christ. He speaks, indeed, of some who would soon introduce grievous heresies and corruptions of Christianity; but for himself he has nothing to add to his former teaching; he is only anxious that it should be remembered, and practically turned to account.

Lastly, Christ's beloved disciple; he who lived so long that some of the brethren supposed that he was never to die at all; he who in an especial manner connects the first age of the Church with the second:—do his epistles, written evidently late in his life,—does his revelation, which so emphatically bears the character of a final declaration of God's will, contain this supposed perfect doctrine of the priesthood and the sacraments? Not one word of either. Written to those who had an unction from the Holy One, and knew all things, to the Church of Christ, with no distinction of priest and layman, St. John's epistle contains no new commandment, but the same which the Church had received from the beginning: his gospel is Paul's gospel also; God's infinite love in Christ, Christ dying for us, faith working by love: holiness being the mark of God's people; sin the mark of false brethren. Of priesthoods, of one body of men ministering grace to the rest through certain outward rites which, unless administered by them, lose their efficacy, St. John, like St. Peter and St. Paul, says nothing. Something, indeed, he does say of the spirit of priestcraft, in order to condemn it; there was one Diotrephes who loved to exercise authority, and to cast out of the Church those of God's people who were strangers to his particular portion of it; and reproved those who knew better the largeness of Christian charity. But Diotrephes, the true prototype of priestly and fanatical presumption, is condemned by Christ's beloved Apostle, as prating against him with malicious words; as disobeying by his bigotry the authority of the loving apostles of Christ Jesus.

The latest writings, then, of these three great Apostles—Paul, Peter, and John—contain no traces of any other or more mysterious doctrines than they had received from our Lord and taught to their first converts at the beginning of the gospel. And the expressions already alluded to in the Epistle to the Hebrews, like the whole of that epistle, are, in fact, directly opposed to the notion of a more mystical Christianity, which was to be the reward of a due improvement of the first principles of Christian knowledge already communicated. The "perfection" of which the writer speaks as opposed to the principles or the elementary doctrine of Christ, is an understanding that the law, its priesthood, and its sacrifices were no longer necessary, inasmuch as Christ, by his eternal priesthood and one sacrifice, had done effectually that work which they could but typically foreshadow. It is well known that the Jewish Christians still observed the ceremonial law; and the Apostles sanctioned this, not only to avoid unnecessary offence to the unbelieving Jews, but also because the converts themselves would have been shocked at the notion of renouncing it. St. Paul, however, and those who followed him, were well aware that this observance of the law was very apt to be coupled with a belief of its necessity in a spiritual point of view, and therefore they represent the full-grown Christian as one who feels the unimportance of all Jewish ceremonies, and who places his whole reliance upon Christ. "Let us, as many as are perfect," says St. Paul to the Philippians, "be thus minded:" where his meaning is exactly the same with that of the epistle to the Hebrews, where he speaks of going on unto perfection. So far, then, was the perfection of Christian doctrine from consisting in the belief in a human priesthood, and in the mystic virtue of outward ordinances, that it was the very opposite of this, and consisted in clearly understanding that Christ's death and resurrection had rendered all priesthoods, sacrifices, and ceremonies, for the time to come, unimportant. It was because this perfection was not generally attained to, because the minds of so many Christians could not embrace principles so pure, that the doctrine of the priesthood and the sacraments gradually made its way into the Church, as the natural successor of Judaism. For when the Jewish temple and sacrifices were destroyed, those Christians who had till then regarded them as important parts of Christianity, were naturally led to substitute another priesthood and another sacrifice of the same sort in the place of those which they had lost: and as they had joined the Levitical priesthood with that of Christ, and the daily sacrifices of the law with his sacrifice, so afterwards, in the same spirit, they made a new priesthood out of the Christian ministry, and a new sacrifice out of the communion of the Lord's Supper.

It may be safely said, that whatever we find in

the New Testament, as to a gradual communication of Christian truth, relates to this one point: that the disciples were to be led on gently to a full sense of the unimportance of the ceremonies of the Jewish law. Christianity was given complete, as to its own truths, from the beginning of the gospel: but the absolute sufficiency of these truths, and the needlessness of any other system as joined with them, was to be learned only by degrees; and, unhappily, it never was learned fully. The perfection of which the epistle to the Hebrews speaks as not having been yet reached by those to whom the author was writing, was, by the great mass of the Church, never reached at all. The errors of the Judaizers continued, and assumed a shape far more mischievous; because the Judaism of the succession priesthood, and the sacrifice of the communion, did not, like the older Judaism, simply exist by the side of pure Christianity, but incorporated itself with Christianity, and destroyed Christian truths to substitute in the place of them its own falsehood.

Thus, then, as the Scriptures wholly disclaim these notions of a human priesthood, as the perfection of knowledge to which they would have us aspire consists in rejecting such notions wholly; it is strictly, as I said, superfluous to inquire into the opinions of early Christian writers, because, if these upheld the doctrine of the priesthood ever so strongly, it would but show that the state of mind of which the epistle to the Hebrews complains, was afterwards more universal and more remote from Christian perfection. But it is satisfactory to find that this was not so; that although the germs of the mischief may be here and there discernible, yet that the doctrine of the Apostles was in the main faithfully taught by those who, in point of time, came nearest to them; that it needed more than one generation to corrupt so deeply the perfect purity of Christian truth.

Our inquiry will not be a very long one. For when that favourite expression with some, "the voice of Christian antiquity," is analyzed, it appears that, besides the writers of the New Testament, the first century and a half of the Christian era produced no more than ten writers, or, if we include Justin Martyr, eleven. These were all whom Jerome could discover, although he professes to give a complete list of the Christian writers from the earliest times, and even swells it with the names of Josephus, Philo-Judæus, Justus of Tiberias, who was also a Jewish writer, and L. Seneca.

The ten writers of Jerome's list are the following: Barnabas, Hermas, Clemens of Rome, Ignatius, Polycarp, Papias, Quadratus, Aristides, Agrippa, and Hegesippus. Of this number the works of the five last have perished, with the exception of a few passages preserved in quotations by other writers. But Quadratus and Aristides were only known to Jerome himself as the authors of two apologies in behalf of Christianity, addressed to the emperor Hadrian; and Agrippa's works were an answer to the heretic Basilides, of which it is not certain that it was extant in the time of Jerome. Of Polycarp and Ignatius, Jerome knew no other works than those which we still possess under their names; that is, Polycarp's epistle to the Philippians, and the seven epistles of Ignatius: 1, to the Ephesians; 2, to the Magnesians; 3, to the Trallensians; 4, to the Romans; 5, to the Philadelphians; 6, to the Smyrnæans; and 7, to Polycarp. Barnabas, also, and Hermas were known to Jerome only by the Epistle of the former, and by the Shepherd of the latter, both of which we possess. And the only undisputed work of Clemens, his epistle to the Corinthians, is also still in existence. The only important remains of Christian antiquity which Jerome possessed, and which are lost to us, are therefore the Apologies of Quadratus and Aristides, the Ecclesiastical History of Hegesippus, and Papias's five books, entitled "A Setting Forth of the Words of the Lord." "Ἔκθεσις λόγων Κυρίου.

It is not my present purpose to inquire into the genuineness of the epistle of Barnabas, or of the other writings of the so-called Apostolical fathers. I am willing for the present to assume that they are genuine, because I wish to meet the advocates of the priesthood on their own ground; and I contend that their system can no more be derived from the reputed works of the earliest Christian writers, than from the Scriptures themselves. If there be no works remaining of the Christian writers of the first century and a half, it is idle to talk about a tradition running back to the very times of the Apostles; the links of the chain are wanting in the very most important part, and the wide gap between the Apostles and Justin Martyr must resist every attempt to connect the opinions of the end of the second century with the Christianity of the Apostolical age.

I. The epistle of Barnabas is directed mainly against the notions of the Judaizers. The writer is so earnest against the observance of the Jewish law by Christians, that he ascribes a figurative and spiritual meaning to all those passages in the Old Testament which enjoin the several ceremonies of the Jewish ritual. Even circumcision, he contends, meant the circumcision of the heart, and not the outward rite; and after stating an objection to this view of it, in the words of a supposed opponent, who observes, "that the Jews were circumcised as a seal of their covenant," he replies, " But the Syrians and Arabians, and the idol priests generally, use circumcision. Are they also, then, partakers of God's covenants?" A writer who would so little admit outward ceremonies as an essential part of the Jewish religion, was not likely to regard them as essential in Christianity. There is, accordingly, not a single word about any Christian ceremonial, whether of temple, priesthood, or offering; he knows nothing of the Eucharist as the unbloody sacrifice of the new law, to be offered only by the new priesthood; he only knows of the sacrifice once offered by Christ, of the whole Church as the spiritual temple of God. It is true he speaks of baptism under the name of "water," and applies to it several passages in the Old Testament, which speak of "streams of water," "living springs," &c. And from these expressions, it might be supposed that he was laying a stress on the outward act of baptism. For instance, the following words might be quoted as identifying baptism with regeneration :—" We go down to the water full of sins and filthiness, and we come up with our hearts bringing forth fruit; having fear and hope towards Jesus through the Spirit." This and other such passages serve admirably well, when quoted separately, to make it appear that Barnabas held the Judaizing notions of the mystical virtue of the sacraments: but when we compare his strong language, as to the utter worthlessness of the outward act of circumcision, and as to the circumcision of the heart being the only thing intended by the commandment, it is quite clear that, by parity of reasoning, the whole importance of baptism in his eyes must have consisted in the real change of heart which it implied, and the change of life of which it was the beginning, and that the ceremony of baptizing with water was merely a symbol of the great and important change which a man underwent in passing from a state of heathenism to Christianity. In this sense, baptism, as synonymous with an admission to the benefits and promises of the Christian Church, could not be spoken of too highly; it was truly the turning-point of a man's whole existence from evil to good. And in the time of Barnabas, when the real change involved in the act of baptism was so striking, and the superstitions connected with it had not as yet had full time to grow up, any one might speak of it as Barnabas has spoken, without suspecting that his words could be misinterpreted. St. Peter himself says, " Baptism does now save us;" and it seems to me rather an instance of God's abundant goodness, to hinder the Scriptures from giving any countenance to the Judaizing superstitions, than a necessary caution on the writer's part to save himself from misinterpretation, when he adds expressly, "Not the putting away the filth of the flesh, but the answer of a good conscience towards God."

It should be always remembered, that the superstition of the Judaizers consists not in their reverence for the sacraments, which Christ appointed as great instruments of good to his Church, but in their having drawn off men's attention from the important part both of Baptism and the Lord's Supper to that which is external: to regard God's grace not as conveyed by them morally, because the joining Christ's Church in the first instance, and the constantly refreshing our communion with it afterwards, are actions highly beneficial to our moral nature; but as conveyed by them after the manner of a charm, the virtue being communicated by the water and the bread and wine, in consequence of a virtue first communicated to them by certain words of consecration pronounced by a priest. It is the famous " accedit verbum ad elementum et fit sacramentum," which contains the essence of the unchristian and most mischievous view of the sacraments entertained by the Romish and Anglican popery. And, in order to show that the early Christian writers favour this notion, it is not enough to show that they speak strongly of the benefits of the sacraments, for in this the Scriptures and almost all true Christians would agree with them : but it must farther be made evident that they lay the stress on the virtue communicated by the outward elements, after those elements have been first consecrated by certain formal words repeated by a priest. Unless they can be proved to hold this, we may interpret their language rather as agreeing with that of Christ and his apostles, than as countenancing the superstition of the Judaizers.

From the epistle of Barnabas, I pass to that of Clemens Romanus.

II. There is nothing in Clemens, either on the subject of Baptism or of the Lord's Supper, or of a priesthood. But there are one or two passages which have been often quoted as asserting what is called apostolical succession; and these, therefore, it will be proper to examine. As before, in the case of the epistle of Barnabas, I am assuming the genuineness of the epistle of Clemens, and also its freedom from interpolation.

It is difficult, unfortunately, notwithstanding the length of this work, to learn from it with any clearness the exact nature of the circumstances to which it refers. It complains, indeed, largely of the mischiefs of quarrelling and pride; but it does not state what was the occasion of quarrel, nor what were the views and objects of the party which disturbed the peace of the Church. They are spoken of as "a few," ὀλίγα πρόσωπα; and they are blamed as "lifting themselves up over Christ's flock," ἐπαιρομένων ἐπὶ τὸ ποίμνιον τοῦ Χριστοῦ, at the same time that they were disparaging the authority of the lawful elders of the Church. Some of the elders had been actually displaced, and for no fault of theirs; and those through whom they had been expelled had gained a great authority in their room. These last Clement exhorts to give up their power, to do the bidding of the congregation, τὰ προστασσόμενα ὑπὸ τοῦ πλήθους, and to imitate the example of many worthy kings and rulers of the Gentiles, who had left their own countries rather than be the occasion of contention or civil war.

All this is to us exceedingly vague; it reminds us something of the tyrants of the old Greek commonwealths, establishing themselves on the overthrow of the old aristocracies. It bears some resemblance to the picture drawn by St. Paul of his Judaizing opponents in this very Church of Corinth, who depreciated or denied his authority, and trampled themselves upon the mass of the congregation with the utmost insolence[a]. It would perfectly suit an attempt made on the part of one or two ambitious individuals to establish the despotism of a single bishop, instead of the mild authority of the whole body of elders: for certain it is that Clement, like St. Paul, recognises no one bishop, in the later sense of the term, as ruling

[a] See II. Corinth. xi. 20.

the Church of Corinth; the government is vested in a certain number of bishops or elders, called indifferently by either name, who, together with the inferior ministers, διάκονοι, or in the language of the Athenian constitution, ὑπήρεται, constitute all the officers of the Christian society.

With this uncertainty as to the precise nature of the disturbance in the Corinthian Church, we cannot tell with what extent or with what limits to understand the particular passage of Clement's epistle, which is supposed to uphold the doctrine of the so-called apostolical succession. He refers to the minute rules of the Jewish Church; to its division of offices, and its stated seasons and places of worship; and he infers from this, that each man in the Christian Church should keep his own station and order with equal strictness. The Apostles, he says, appointed everywhere the first bishops and deacons, ἐπισκόπους καὶ διακόνους, in the several Churches which they founded. They wished to obviate disputes about the government, and therefore they not only appointed the first bishops and deacons, but also appointed a succession, ἐπινομήν, that when the first bishops were dead, other tried men should succeed to their office. "Those, then," proceeds Clement, "who were appointed by the Apostles, or afterwards (μεταξύ), by other tried and approved men (ἐλλογίμων), with the consent of the whole Church;

those who ministered unblamably to Christ's flock with humility, gently, and in no spirit of sordid gain (ἀβαναύσως), and whose worth has many times been attested by the whole Church—these, we think, are not justly expelled from their ministry; for it will be no small sin to us, if they who unblamably and holily offered their gifts to God, be cast out from their bishoprics." Such is the famous passage in which Clement is supposed to maintain the indefeasible right of bishops appointed by apostolical succession to exercise government over the Church for ever.

It is manifest, in the first place, that Clement's words are not general and prospective, but had reference to a particular case actually before him. He was thinking of something present and special, and had evidently no thought of laying down a general law for all times and places. Now, I am very far from saying that the words of a wise man, on a particular case, cannot contain any truth of general application; of course they can, and generally do: but as he did not utter them as general, their bearing on any universal truth is indirect rather than direct; that is, we may conclude that he would have applied them generally, so far as the particular case before him was a faithful representative of all future cases; but if it differed in any remarkable points from future cases, then we have no right to make them general: in other words, we have no right to make him draw the same conclusion, where the premises are manifestly different.

Now the premises in Clement's case lead justly enough, assuming them for the present to be true in fact, to his conclusion. Good elders, appointed by worthy men, who had themselves been appointed by the apostles, appointed with the consent of the whole Church, whose worth the whole Church had often attested, and who had discharged their ministry unblamably, gently, and uncorruptly, ought not to be deprived of their office. I am not aware that the strongest opponent of priestly tyranny would refuse his hearty assent to this proposition of Clement.

But now, instead of Clement's own premises, let us substitute others. " Bad and foolish elders, appointed by others neither wiser nor better, which others derived their own appointment from no purer source,—proud and foolish elders, in whose appointment the whole Church had had no voice at all, nor had ever attested their worth, but felt their evil,—elders who had discharged their office offensively, arrogantly, rapaciously,"—shall there be no power in the Church to deprive such of their office, and to commit the power which they abuse, and have long abused, to other hands? Or, is

Clement's conclusion still to hold, although of the premises from which he derived it, there is not left in this new case a single one remaining?

It must not be denied, however, that a comparison which Clement uses in this part of his epistle, may seem to imply that he regarded the government of the Church as a thing fixed once for all, and not to be altered under any circumstances. He refers to the selection of the family of Aaron to hold the priest's office, as a parallel case to the appointment of the first bishops by the Apostles; and as the priesthood remained in Aaron's family to the end of the Jewish dispensation, without any reference to the worthiness of the individuals of that family in any one generation, so it might be argued that, in Clement's notions, the personal worthiness or unworthiness of the individual bishops had nothing to do with the question; their right to govern the Church was derived solely from their Apostolical succession.

Now, if Clement had been arguing in the abstract against the right of deposing any bishop or elder, and had then referred to the law of the Jewish priesthood, there could have been no doubt as to his meaning. But this is precisely one of those points in which the particular occasion of his argument makes his meaning, as to the general applicability of his comparison, doubtful. If he felt that bishops or elders had been factiously and unjustly deposed, when they had been appointed to their office either immediately by the Apostles, or at only one remove, by those who had themselves received their office from the Apostles, the deposition of such men so appointed could not but seem to him an interference with a divine authority; and he would have looked upon their power, so unjustly assailed, as resting on God's ordinance, as much as the exclusive possession of the priesthood by the family of Aaron.

But it is impossible to argue justly from this passage, that if Clement had lived fifteen or sixteen centuries later, and had seen the bishops of the Church in a wholly different position from that of the bishops of the church of Corinth, he would have equally maintained their indefeasibility, and considered the Levitical priesthood an exactly parallel case. For the continuance of the priesthood in the same family was not a consequence simply of the original divine appointment of Aaron, but followed from the universal notion of the eastern world, and of much of the western, that priesthoods must be hereditary. God appointed Moses to be the prophet and ruler of his people, and Moses after him appointed Joshua; but the divine appointment went on farther, because the prophets' and judges' offices were not necessarily to depend upon succession, and the Israelites were not bound to choose for their judges the posterity of either

Moses or Joshua. Now the Christian ministry would undoubtedly resemble the judges and prophets of the Israelites rather than their priests; and therefore an original divine appointment would not imply the necessity of a perpetual succession. The succession here would, as to its divine authority, die out naturally in the course of time, just as the Roman lawyers held that collateral consanguinity expired in the eighth generation; it being impossible to suppose that the virtue of the original descent from a common ancestor could exist beyond that period. Thus, the elders appointed immediately, or at one or two removes, by the Apostles, might truly be said to hold their offices, like Joshua, by divine appointment; and they might as truly be said to have been chosen by God, as Aaron was chosen to be the priest, rather than a man of any other family or any other tribe. And the reason why the succession was not to be perpetual in the case of the judge of Israel and the Christian bishops was this, that unless each generation was as highly gifted by God as Moses and Joshua, or as the Christian Apostles, the wisdom of their original choice of successors would be impaired continually by fresh mixtures of human folly or passion; so that, as in the case of collateral consanguinity, all its virtue must necessarily be lost after the lapse of a certain interval of time. This is the plain analogy and reason which makes it probable that Clement would not have considered any bishops of the Church, after the lapse of a century, to be the successors of the Apostles, except so far as they resembled them in their lives and doctrine.

Nothing is less satisfactory than an argumentum ad hominem; and therefore I have chosen to consider this passage of Clement with a view simply to the truth of the case, and not merely to the silencing or embarrassing an adversary. Otherwise it is most true that the actual episcopacy of the Christian Church, for many centuries, can derive no support from the epistle of Clement. An aristocracy and a monarchy are not so precisely identical that the government of a single bishop can claim to be of divine authority, because the Apostles appointed in each church a certain number of bishops or elders. Nor can it be shown that if the ordination by bishops, one or more, be necessary, the consent of the whole church, which was no less a part of the primitive appointments, may be laid aside as a thing wholly indifferent. But it is a poor triumph merely to expose an opponent's inconsistencies: it is far better to show, simply, that Clement's words — 1st, grew out of a particular occasion; 2nd, that the bishops to whose deposition he objected were good men, who had discharged their office well, and who had been appointed with the consent of the whole church; 3rd, that they were really and bonâ fide the Apostles' successors, being no farther removed from them than the virtue of the Apostles' original choice might fairly be supposed to reach; 4th, that the virtue of that choice necessarily dying out in time, it can never be proved that he who upheld its authority when it really existed, would therefore imagine it to exist when it was really lost; and 5th, that the cases of Moses and Joshua, and the essential difference between a priesthood and an office of prophet or ruler, make it clear that indefeasible succession does not flow from an original divine appointment in the latter case, because it accompanied it in the former.

Finally, it must be remembered that Clement speaks of the Christian ministers as bishops and elders, not as priests. It is not a little curious that, just at that period when the notion of original Apostolical appointment could no longer be applied to make out a virtual succession for the Christian ministers as prophets or rulers, their office began to be represented as a priesthood; that so the succession, which was inapplicable to them in their real character, might be claimed for them under this new and unchristian title.

III. The "Shepherd" of Hermas contains no mention of the Lord's Supper, nor of a priesthood, nor of a succession of ministers, nor of a mystical virtue communicated to the elements in the sacraments by a certain form of words. Baptism, as the admission into the Christian Church, and as equivalent to the obtaining a knowledge of Christ, is indeed strongly insisted on in a remarkable passage, in which Hermas says that the Apostles after their deaths went down into the place of the dead, and preached there to the good men of former ages, and taught them the name of the Lord Jesus, and baptized them; and that then, having received the seal of the Son of God, they arose perfect and fit for God's kingdom. "For," says Hermas, "they had died full of righteousness, and in a state of great purity, only they had not received this seal." I am far from saying that there is not some superstition involved in this; but still the notion is, that the knowledge of the name of Christ was necessary, the seal of which is baptism: the stress is laid on the knowing Christ, and belonging to his Church, not on the mere outward rite of baptizing by water.

IV. The pure and simple epistle of Polycarp is as free from all taint of the corrupt doctrine of a priesthood, and the mystical virtue of the sacraments, as those of the Apostles themselves. He dwells on the relative duties of the several members of the Christian Church, and calls upon the younger men to abstain from all evil lusts, and to be subject to their elders and deacons as unto God and Christ. So St. Paul had desired slaves to obey their masters, and wives to be subject to their own husbands, as unto the Lord. But this is very different from the exaggerated language of Ignatius, and the pretended Apostolical constitutions; and the obedience to the elders and deacons is clearly connected, in Polycarp's mind, with obedience to the law of Christ which they taught, as opposed to the evil lusts from which he wishes all Christian people to turn aside.

V. The epistle of Ignatius to the Romans, assuming as before its genuineness, and not entering into the question whether the longer or the shorter version of it be the original, contains nothing that bears directly on our present subject. One passage, however, may be noticed, as showing that Ignatius understood aright the language of our Lord, recorded in St. John vi., respecting the eating his flesh, and the drinking his blood. "I have no pleasure," says Ignatius, "in corruptible food, nor in this life's pleasures: my wish is for the bread of God, the bread of heaven, the bread of life, that is, the flesh of Jesus Christ, the Son of God, who became afterwards of the seed of David and of Abraham. And the drink which I desire is his blood; which is love incorruptible and life eternal."

Now it should be remembered that Ignatius, in the whole of this epistle, is breathing an earnest desire for martyrdom. He is impatient to arrive at Rome, that he may be torn to pieces by the wild beasts, and so may be for ever with Christ. It is impossible, then, that he can have thought of the communion of the Lord's Supper, when he speaks of the body and blood of Christ: he speaks rather of that perfect communion with Christ in heaven, of which the Lord's Supper was intended, amongst other things, to be the symbol.

It has been one of the most pernicious of all corruptions of Scripture, to understand certain passages as referring to the sacraments, which refer really to those things of which the sacraments are the signs. They are therefore coordinate with the sacraments, pointing in word, as the sacraments do in emblematic action, to the same reality; but not subordinate to the sacraments, nor by any means pointing to them as to the reality, which is something distinct from them and above them.

When our Lord declares, "Whoso eateth my flesh and drinketh my blood hath eternal life, and I will raise him up at the last day; for my flesh is meat indeed, and my blood is drink indeed," it is evident that here is the self-same truth contemplated which our Lord had also in view when he said, "Take, eat, this is my body:" and "Drink ye all of this, for this is my blood of the New Testament, which is shed for many for the remission of sins." There is the self-same truth contemplated, namely, that the closest possible communion of the soul with Christ, and the making him, in all his various relations of Prophet, King, Saviour, and Lord, the soul's daily food, was essential to man's salvation. This great truth our Lord expressed, according to his usual manner, in figurative words; he expressed it also in figurative action. He not only said, "My flesh is meat indeed, and my blood is drink indeed;" but he embodied the words in action; he commanded us to eat as it were his flesh, and to drink his blood, in the bread and wine of the Lord's Supper. But to suppose that the stress was laid on the literal eating of the bread and drinking of the cup, that by that figurative act the great moral reality which it imaged forth symbolically would be ipso facto attained, is a misrepresentation precisely of the same kind as that which he so strongly condemns in his disciples, when they understood his words, to beware of the leaven of the Pharisees, as a charge to beware literally of a particular sort of bread.

Thus again, the summary of the tenth chapter of the first epistle to the Corinthians, as given in our English Bibles, runs thus: "The Jews' sacraments types of ours." Here is the self-same error, of making the outward rites or facts of the Jewish religion *subordinate* to the outward rites of ours, instead of regarding them both as *coordinate with one another,* and *subordinate* to some spiritual reality, of which both alike are but signs. In the passage referred to, St. Paul is showing that outward rites are no security for the existence of the real thing which they typify. Christians have been baptized with water, as an introduction into Christ's service; the Israelites passed through water also, as an introduction to their becoming God's people and receiving his law. Christians eat bread and drink wine, in token of their being united to their Lord and Saviour; and so the Israelites ate manna and drank of the rock, that manna and rock representing Christ their Lord, who was with them on all their way, just as the bread and the wine of the Lord's Supper represent him now. But Israel, notwithstanding these outward tokens of their belonging to God and depending on him, sinned and fell; and notwithstanding our outward tokens, the same may be our case if we are not watchful. It is altering the whole scope of the passage to say that it represents the Jews' sacraments as types of ours; as if our sacraments, any more than theirs, were necessarily or in themselves a reality. The drift of the passage is not to magnify the sacraments, but to prevent us from superstitiously trusting to them. The Jews had their sacraments, as we have ours, and both are types of the same thing; but the type in their case did not prevent them from forfeiting the substance, neither will it in ours.

So again, when St. John records so earnestly his beholding the blood and water flowing out from Christ's side, and when in his epistle, in manifest allusion to the same thing, he says, "This is he who came by water and blood, even Jesus Christ; not by water only, but by water and blood:" it makes the whole difference between Christianity and the great corruption of it, whether we understand these words as *coordinate with* Baptism and the Lord's Supper, or as *subordinate to* them; whether we say that they refer to the two sacraments, or that they refer to those great truths which the two sacraments also were designed to image forth in emblematic action; that repentance towards God, and faith in the blood of our Lord Jesus Christ, are the sum and substance of Christianity.

Finally, the memorable words of our Lord himself to Nicodemus, "Except a man be born of water and of the Spirit, he cannot enter into the kingdom of God," contain, perhaps, the same figure in words that Baptism contains in action, although even this is not certain, but are not meant to refer to the outward rite of Baptism as the thing *indispensable*. They are coordinate with Baptism, it may be, but not subordinate to it.

The same obvious reason which led the Jews, in common with many other people, to adopt the rite of washing the body as symbolical of the washing or cleansing of the soul from sin, led our Lord to express this cleansiag of the soul by the term "water." A man must repent of his past evil life, and receive the grace of the Holy Spirit, to enable him for the future to lead a new life, before he can enter into the kingdom of heaven. And if I am asked why I do not take the word "water" literally, according to Hooker's canon of criticism, when he says that "in the interpretation of Holy Scripture, that sense which is nearest the letter is commonly the safest," I answer, that such a canon as applied to a collection of works, so different in point of style as those of the Scriptures, is at once ridiculous. In the simple narratives of the historical books, Hooker's rule will hold; in the prophetical and poetical books, it would be the very worst rule that we could follow. Now, our Lord's discourses, as recorded by St. John, are eminently parabolical; his language, both when speaking to the Jews and to his own disciples, is continually figurative. Hence the mingled surprise and pleasure of his disciples, when, towards the close of his last conversation with them, he dropped his usual style and expressed himself without any figure. "Lo! now speakest thou plainly, and speakest no proverb."

He spake of water to the woman of Samaria, and she, adopting Hooker's rule, understood him literally: "Lord, give me this water, that I thirst not, neither come hither to draw." Was this, indeed, the true sense of his words; or was it so utterly mistaken as to lead to the extreme of folly and profaneness? And yet, some think, that to interpret in a similar manner his words to Nicodemus is neither foolish nor profane, but rather that to interpret them otherwise is to explain away the words of Scripture! Explaining away the words of Scripture! when we make them refer to something spiritual and not bodily; to a reality, not to a symbol; to a moral act, not to a ceremony!

But why should we scruple to understand our Lord's words of water, literally, when we know that he did on one occasion tell a blind man to go and wash in the pool of Siloam; and that the man went, and washed, and came seeing? This, too, is one of Hooker's comparisons, in that same fifth book of his Ecclesiastical Polity from which so many unwise and unfair arguments have been quoted as the words of impartiality and wisdom. Is it in the slightest degree a parallel case, that because a bodily application was prescribed as a cure for a bodily disease, it should therefore cure a disease of the soul? It is idle to say that we do not understand the laws of body and spirit, and that God can affect both our bodies and spirits by whatever kind of instruments he chooses. The argument from human ignorance, most just and useful within certain limits, is by fanatics often used so awkwardly as to lead to the conclusions of the wildest scepticism. It is true, that we understand very little of the laws of body and spirit, still the very notions of body and spirit imply a wide difference between them; and, so far as we do know or understand of either, our knowledge is derived from different sciences, and we find them to be subjected to different laws. If there is no truth in all this; if we do not know enough to warrant us in saying that wisdom is not to be gained by bodily exercise, nor charity by eating any particular kind of food, then we have no grounds for knowing or believing anything; least of all can we think that we are living in the world of the God of truth and love, if we have no grasp upon truth whatsoever, and have no means by which we may reasonably assure ourselves even that God is.

But, not to wander into any more remote inquiry, it is sufficient for the present to say that the Scriptures fully recognise the authority of what may be called our common-sense notions of good and evil, of reasonableness and absurdity. And when fanaticism, striving to render all truth uncertain, that so its own falsehoods may have the better chance of being received, and pushing to extravagance the famous sentiment of Pascal, "La raison confond les dogmatistes," would endeavour to persuade us, that we can have no sure reliance either on the evidence of our senses or of our reason, that we do not know what is or what is not; our answer will be, that our convictions do not rest on any fond presumption as to our own power of discerning truth, but on our faith that God will not suffer us to be deceived by trusting to his appointed witnesses. Truth in itself we have, it may be, no power to grasp: it may be possible, if you will, that in another state of being, the surest conclusions of our senses and of our reason may be found to have been abstractedly erroneous. But in the meanwhile, in this our present state of being, they are true to us; they are the language to which God has adapted our present nature. By distrusting it, we shall disobey him and be lost in endless error; by believing it, we shall resign ourselves to his guidance, and shall attain, if not truth in itself, yet that only image of truth of which we are capable here, and by which alone we can be made capable of arriving at real truth hereafter. It is not rationalism, then, but reason resting on faith, which assures us of the utter incapability of any outward bodily action to produce in us an inward spiritual effect.

Sect. 1. Epistle of Ignatius to the Ephesians

—In this epistle, we find a marked distinction between the bishop or superintendent, ἐπίσκοπος, and πρεσβυτέριον, or the body of elders; whereas in Clement's epistle, as well as in those of St. Paul, ἐπίσκοπος and πρεσβύτερος are synonymous terms. There are also several passages, enjoining obedience to the bishop and to the body of elders; and in one place Ignatius says, "Ye should regard your Bishop as the Lord himself."[a] But our Lord had said to his disciples, "He that receiveth you receiveth me;" and St. Paul had said, even with regard to the Heathen magistracies, "Whosoever resisteth the power resisteth the ordinance of God." St. Paul also, as we have seen, enjoins Christians no less earnestly to obey those who were set over them; and that Christianity recognises a power of government in the Church, and requires of all individual Christians that they should be obedient to those invested with this government, we have already shown at large. But government is not priesthood, and neither these passages of Ignatius, nor those quoted before from St. Paul, contain one word to show that the bishops and elders of the Christian Church were priests as well as rulers.

It may be worth our while, however, to see what it was which induced Ignatius thus strongly to urge the duty of obedience to the bishop and the

[a] [St. Ignat. ad. Ephes. vi.]

elders; because, if we understand this rightly, we shall find much excuse, at any rate, for certain strong expressions, which otherwise, taken apart from the context, and as meant merely to convey a high notion of the episcopal dignity, breathe a language very different from that of St. Peter and St. Paul. Every great reform which has taken place in human society has contained, among its nominal advocates, men who are morally the extreme opposites of each other; some being the very best and noblest of their kind, and others the vilest. And it is these last who explain the otherwise monstrous fact, that among the opponents of every reform, there are to be found also, along with the lowest and most wicked of mankind, some few of the loftiest and the purest; men who look at the evil supporters of the reform, and for their sakes dread it and abhor it. Now, even Christianity itself shared this common lot of all great moral changes; perfect as it was in itself, its nominal adherents were often neither wise nor good, but took part with it for its negative side, not for its positive: advocating it so far as it destroyed what was already in existence, but having no sympathy with that better state of things which it proposed to set up in the room of the old. For when the 'Church began to show its wide range of action, and its singular efficacy, all who longed to see the existing system overthrown, rallied themselves round its assailant. Here, they thought, was a power which they could use for the accomplishment of their purpose: when this should have first cleared the ground of the thickets which encumbered it, it would be for them to sow in the vacant soil their own favourite seed.

Now let any one, who knows what the Roman Empire was in the first century of the Christian era, imagine to himself the monstrous forms of opinion and practice which a state of society so diseased could not fail to engender. All varieties of ancient and foreign superstition existed, together with the worst extremity of unprincipled scepticism; while in practice the unquelled barbarism of the ruder provinces, and the selfish cruelty fostered by long and bloody civil wars, had provided a fearful mass of the fiercer passions; and the unrestrained dissoluteness of a thoroughly corrupt society was a source no less abundant of every thing most shameless in sensuality. These seemingly incongruous evils, superstition and scepticism, ferocity and sensual profligacy, when from any particular circumstances they turned against the monster society which had bred them, and began to seek its destruction, often sheltered themselves under the name of Christianity, and were the heresies of the first age of the Christian Church.

That this was so would be, I think, sufficiently

proved by that well-known passage of Tacitus, in which he describes the Christians as " per flagitia invisos," and their system as one amongst things " atrocia et pudenda."[b] We know full well that Tacitus would not have applied such language to true Christians, and to true Christianity. We know that no wise and good heathen ever did apply such terms to either. But Tacitus's testimony, and the very fact itself that the Christian name was generally odious, as connected with all manner of wickedness, are quite sufficient to prove that there were nominal Christians, whose rites and whose practices were at once licentious and dangerous to public order; who formed a secret society, fraught with mischief to the morals of individuals, no less than to the tranquillity of the state.

We are not left, however, to the mere testimony of Tacitus; the highest Christian authorities confirm the same thing. These combined features, sensual profligacy and lawless turbulence, appear exactly in the portraits of the heretical Christians drawn by St. Jude, and by St. Peter in his second epistle. Nor does the disputed genuineness of these two writings affect the question, for whether written by Apostles or no, it has never been doubted that they are the works of Christians in the first century; and that is sufficient for our purpose. The account given by Eusebius of the gross licen-

[b] [Tac Ann. xv. 44.]

tiousness of the Nicolaitans, agreeing with the strong language used concerning them in the Revelation, is another evidence to the same effect. I think also that the same thing is implied in the first epistle of St. Peter. Twice in that epistle he admits that the heathens spoke against Christians as evildoers; and he by no means denies altogether the truth of the charge, but rather urges those to whom he was writing to show that in their case it was false. His question, "Who is he that will harm you, if ye become ($\gamma \acute{\epsilon} \nu \eta \sigma \theta \epsilon$) followers of that which is good?" and his saying, "Let none of you suffer as a murderer, or thief, or evildoer,"[a] appear to show that a portion at least of the sufferings of persons calling themselves Christians, had been really the just consequence of their crimes: and it is remarkable that here, too, the command "to abstain from fleshly lusts," is followed immediately by the command "to obey the laws and government;"[b] as if the Apostle was regarding the very same characters who are described in his second epistle,—men at once licentious and anarchical.

In St Paul's epistles, we find no less frequent indication that there existed many within the Church, whose principles and lives were altogether unchristian. The well-known passage in 2 Timothy iii. 1—8, refers, indeed, rather to a time imme-

[a] [1 St. Peter, iii. 13; iv. 15.] [b] [Ibid., ii. 11, 13.]

diately following than to one past or present; still it was verified before the close of the first century. But the union of superstition and profligacy is described as a thing actually existing in the Church in the epistle to the Philippians, iii. 18, 19, and again in the epistle to the Galatians, vi. 12, 13; and it appears above all in the Judaizers, so often referred to in the epistles to the Corinthians. It is evident, too, from the peculiar language twice used in declaring the sinfulness of licentious pleasure, "Be not deceived,"—"He therefore that despiseth, despiseth not man but God,"[a] that there were some who would not listen to the Apostle in this matter, and who tried to persuade their fellow-Christians that he was imposing on them a yoke needlessly rigid. Finally, the corruptors of true Christianity, whom Titus was sent to Crete to check, were vain talkers and deceivers, giving heed to Jewish fables and human traditions, and at the same time denying God in their lives, and being "abominable" (βδελυκτοί), "and to every good work reprobate" (ἀδόκιμοι,)—"of no account and worthless."[b]

These passages might be greatly multiplied, but what has already been quoted is sufficient for our purpose. A great point is gained, when we understand that the heresies condemned by the Apostles

[a] [1 Corinthians, vi. 9; 1 Thessalonians, iv. 8.]
[b] [Titus, i. 10—16.]

were not mere erroneous opinions on some theoretical truth, but absolute perversions of Christian holiness; that they were not so much false as wicked. And further, where there was a false opinion in the heresy, it was of so monstrous a character, and so directly connected with profligacy of life, that it admits of no comparison with the so-called heresies of later ages. What should we think of men professing themselves to be Christians, and yet maintaining, as did the Docetæ, that Christ never really died or really rose, or asserting that the resurrection was past already; that is, that in a sense of a rising from the grave to eternal life there was no resurrection at all?

These opinions and principles, and this practice, existed in the early Church, in open defiance of the authority of the Apostles. In the Arian controversy, and in all others which have since arisen among Christians, the question has turned upon the true interpretation of the Apostle's words; but both parties have alike acknowledged, that what the Apostles taught was to be received as the undoubted rule of faith and of action. Not so, however, the real heretics of the first century. St. Paul is continually arguing against adversaries, with whom his bare authority, it is evident, would have weighed nothing. How strong is his expression to Timothy, "All they that are in Asia are turned away from me :"ᵃ—they have followed another view of Christianity as better than mine. And again, in matters of government, we see that Diotrephes, a man evidently of no mean rank in the Church, openly set at nought the authority of St. John.ᵇ Thus it appears that we were in danger, humanly speaking, of having a Christian Church, a society of men baptized in the name of the Lord Jesus, who yet did not acknowledge the authority of Christ's Apostles, and who believed and practised things most opposite to the principles and revelations of true Christianity.

It was therefore no vain superstition, and no wish to establish a priestly dominion, which led Ignatius to insist strongly on agreement with and obedience to the bishop, or which had induced Clement to press the importance of not displacing those elders who had been appointed directly or at one remove by the Apostles themselves. And the view here taken will also account for the otherwise irrelevant language which accompanies such exhortations to obedience. It explains why Polycarp should speak of being subject to the elders and deacons in close connexion with his charge to abstain from fleshly lusts. Καλὸν γὰρ τὸ ἀνακύπτεσθαι ἀπὸ τῶν ἐπιθυμιῶν ἐν τῷ κόσμῳ, ὅτι πᾶσα ἐπιθυμία κατὰ τοῦ πνεύματος στρατεύεται . . . . Διὸ δέον ἀπέχεσθαι ἀπὸ πάντων τούτων, ὑποτασσομένους τοῖς πρεσβυτέ-

---
ᵃ [2 Tim. i. 15.]   ᵇ [3 John, 9.]

ροις καὶ διακόνοις, ὡς Θεῷ καὶ Χριστῷ.[a] Compare our Lord's words with regard to the Scribes and Pharisees:—"The Scribes and Pharisees sit in Moses' seat: all therefore whatsoever they bid you observe, that observe and do."[b] That is, "they are teachers of a true revelation from God, and whatever they bid you observe in their teaching, that do, without regard to the bad characters of those who so teach you." That our Lord directed obedience to them only so far as they taught the commandments of Moses, is clear from this, that he did not obey them himself in those usages which they had engrafted on the law of Moses by their own sole authority. And so Polycarp's command to the young Christians to be subject to their elders and deacons, and to abstain from fleshly lusts, has a direct reference to them as teachers of genuine Christianity, which condemned such indulgences, in opposition to many heretical teachers, and to the general opinion of the heathen world, which regarded them with indifference.

The same reason for enforcing obedience to the bishop appears in the epistle of Ignatius to the Ephesians. The bishop of that church, at the time when this epistle was written, was Onesimus, of whom, personally, Ignatius speaks in very high terms. He commends also Burrhus, a deacon of

---

[a] [St. Polycarp, ad Philipp. v.]
[b] [St. Matthew xxiii. 2, 3.]

the same church, together with Crocus, Euplus, and Fronto, all of them probably holding some station in the government of it. Now, if Ignatius remembered how Paul himself had complained that all they who were in Asia (i. e., the Roman province so called, of which Ephesus was one of the principal cities) were turned away from him, and how especially he had commissioned Timotheus to purify the government of the Ephesian Church, in order to stop the spreading of false and mischievous principles; what wonder is it that, seeing now such a bishop and such a government as he thoroughly approved of, he should urge the Church to the closest union with them, and the strictest obedience to their instructions, as the readiest way of abiding and advancing in the true path of Christian holiness?

Thus, when he speaks of Onesimus as praising the orderliness of the Ephesians,—that they lived according to truth, and that no sect following falsehood dwelt among them,—he adds[a], "For some are wont to carry about their name" (scil., their name of Christians) "falsely and deceitfully, doing deeds unworthy of God: these ye should shun as wild beasts; for they are mad dogs, biting before men are aware: and ye should beware of these, for their madness is hard to cure."[b] And again, "Even your deeds of a fleshly sort are all spiritual, for ye

[a] [St. Ignat. ad Eph. vi.]   [b] [Ibid. vii.]

do all things in Jesus Christ; but I know that some have gone aside from that right way, and have an evil doctrine."ᵃ

This also explains the earnest desire manifested by Ignatius, that the Church should go on in unity. Parties existed bearing the name of Christians, but only serving by their monstrous principles and evil lives to bring that name into dishonour. How closely, then, ought all real Christians to hold together, lest their whole society should fall to pieces! But to the Church, or society of Christians, God's promises were given; Christianity was not meant to be held by a multitude of isolated individuals, but where the lawful government and the majority of a society are, there is the society itself. Hence the strong expression of Ignatius: "Let no man be misled: if a man be not within the altar, he fails of obtaining the bread of God. For if the prayer of one or two be of such force, how much more that of the bishop and of the whole Church? He, then, who joins not with the rest of the Church, he, we may be sure, is proud; . . . . for it is written, 'God resisteth the proud.' Let us be careful then not to resist our bishop, that we may be subject to God."ᵇ We should particularly observe the stress here laid on the prayers of a great number, which is just like the language of St.

ᵃ [St. Ignat. ad Ephes. viii. ix.]
ᵇ [Ibid. v.]

Paul[a]; but it is quite inconsistent with a system of priestcraft, where the numbers of the people signify nothing, but the virtue is supposed to reside in the prayers of the priest. And although the language here used by Ignatius was very liable to abuse, and although Cyprian, and still more the Church writers of later times, have abused it most palpably, yet still, as used by Ignatius himself, it really contains nothing objectionable, if we only take the pains to understand the circumstances of the case. He saw the Church falling to pieces by the formation of various parties whose principles and practice were alike unchristian. The bishops appointed either immediately or at one remove by the Apostles, were upholding the authority of the Apostles' doctrine, and endeavouring to enforce it. Around them, therefore, was the true Church gathered. Here was a genuine apostolical succession; and to this Church, governed by these bishops, Ignatius earnestly exhorts all Christians to adhere, as separation from it was either abandoning Christianity altogether, and substituting in the place of it some monstrous system of error and wickedness; or else it was the indulgence of individual pride or unsocial temper, in separating from the Christian society, and forming a religion for themselves individually. And if the bishops now had been virtually selected by the

[[a] 2 Cor. i. 11; iv, 15.]

Apostles, as men on whom they could depend; or if they were the only teachers who taught true Christianity now, while other ministers, instead of preaching the Gospel, taught Manicheism, or Mohammedanism; or, again, if the bishops and their churches formed such a living Christian society, that separation from them could only be the pride or fantastic spirit of a few individuals; then the sentiments of Ignatius, although expressed according to the temper of the man, with too little qualification, would yet in the main be just and applicable now.

Sect. 2. Epistle to the Smyrnæans.—In this epistle, Ignatius is earnestly writing against those who have been called "Docetæ;" those who contended that our Lord did not really die and rise again, but only seemingly. ($\delta o \kappa \epsilon \hat{\imath} \nu$ $a \vec{v} \tau \grave{o} \nu$ $\pi \epsilon \pi o \nu \theta \acute{\epsilon} \nu a \iota$.) These persons also, he says, were unchristian in their spirit and life: "They have no care for charity, nor for widow nor for orphan, nor for the distressed, nor for the prisoner, nor for the hungry or the thirsty. They abstain from the Eucharist, and from public prayer, because they do not allow that the Eucharist is the flesh of our Saviour Jesus Christ, the flesh which suffered for our sins, which in his goodness the Father raised up."[a]

Now, it is manifest that if this passage bears at all upon the priestly notions of the communion, it

[St. Ignat. ad Smyrn. vi.]

goes the whole length either of transubstantiation, or at least of consubstantiation. If Ignatius meant to condemn the Docetæ for not thinking highly enough of the elements, as they are called, used in the communion; then undoubtedly his words were very incautiously used, if he did not intend his readers to believe that the bread and wine *were* actually the body and blood of Christ. In this case, his authority may be of use to the members of the Church of Rome, in their disputes with those of the Church of England, but cannot be pleaded consistently by us, so long as we profess to abide by our present Articles and Liturgy. But in truth Ignatius objects to the practice of the Docetæ on a very different ground. He complains of their rejection of the symbol as showing that they rejected that reality which it signified. The Communion was intended to keep in memory the death of our Lord, and through our memory to strengthen our faith, and so to make us actually and personally partakers in the benefits of his death. But the Docetæ said that he had not really died, and had made therefore no real sacrifice for us. Faith in what had no real existence must be vain; and the memory of an unreal event must be vain also. Therefore they rejected the Communion, and in so doing they showed that their notions were not the notions of Christ and his Apostles, and his Church. For the Communion had been instituted by Christ to keep alive for ever the remembrance of his death; and this showed that his death was a reality. Now, as the rejection of the Communion followed consistently from their principles, and indeed was required by them; and as they rejected it for the very reason for which Christ had notoriously instituted it, their rejection of it was an evidence that their principles were not the principles of Christianity. This is the drift of Ignatius's argument, and so understood, it is of validity: otherwise, taken as a mere argument upon the nature and inherent virtue of the Eucharistic symbols, it has nothing to do with the opinions of the Docetæ; for it is most certain that thousands of Christians have held the most various notions as to this point, and yet have steadily agreed in celebrating the Communion, and have believed most firmly in the reality and saving effects of that death of Christ which it was appointed to commemorate.

A remarkable passage follows:—"Flee divisions, as the beginning of evils. Follow all of you the bishop, as Jesus Christ followeth his Father; and the estate of the elders as the Apostles; and reverence the deacons as God's ordinance. Let no man do any thing of matters pertaining to the church apart from (or separate from) his bishop. Let that be counted a valid Eucharist, ($\beta\epsilon\beta a i a$,) which is celebrated under the bishop, or under one who shall have received his permission to celebrate it. Wherever the bishop shall appear, there let the people be; in like manner as wheresoever Jesus Christ is, there is the Catholic Church. It is not lawful without the bishop either to baptize, or to celebrate the feast of love; but whatsoever the bishop shall have approved, this is well pleasing to God, that whatever is done may be sure and valid." [a]—ἀσφαλὲς καὶ βέβαιον. And then he goes on:—"It is good to acknowledge God and the bishop. He who honours the bishop is honoured by God; he who does any thing without the knowledge of the bishop, serves the Devil." [b]

The first sensation which we ought to have on reading such a passage as this, is one of gratitude to God, who has not permitted any such language to appear in the writings of the Apostles. In fact, the striking difference between the Scriptures and the early Christian writers, is more observable in what the Scriptures do not contain, than in what they do; for their divine truths are for the most part faithfully copied by the writers who so carefully studied them; but in their freedom from all foolishness and error, they stand altogether alone. Doubtless God's Spirit would not have permitted any Scriptural writer to cast such a snare upon men's consciences as must have been cast by this passage of Ignatius, if it came to us with divine authority. Judged as a mere human writing, there

[a] [Ad Smyrn. viii.]   [b] [Ibid. xi.]

is enough of truth in it, and enough of justification in the circumstances under which it was written, to prevent us from passing a harsh sentence on its author; but blessed be God a thousand times, that no language so exaggerated, and so much more vehement than wise, is to be found in that Word which was designed to be our souls' guide.

I believe fully that Ignatius's horror of divisions n the Christian Church originated in the odious character which those divisions then wore; inasmuch as the separating sects actually separated themselves from the principles of Christianity. I believe, also, that he exalted the authority of the bishops, because he believed that they had been wisely chosen, and that their influence was alone capable of preserving the Church from the evils which surrounded it. It is true, farther, that he was laying down no general and perpetual principle, but speaking to the Christians of Smyrna of his own time, with reference to their own particular bishop. But still the language is unguarded and exaggerated; it forgets that the bishop, like his people, was fallible; that man is not a sufficient stay for other men to rest upon; that if anarchy and faction be evils on the one hand, idolatry of human authority is no less an evil on the other. Compare the tone of this passage with the spirit in which St. Peter expresses himself on the same subject :—" The elders who are among you I exhort, ... to feed the flock of God, ... taking the oversight thereof not by constraint, but willingly; not for filthy lucre, but of a ready mind; neither as being lords over God's heritage, but being ensamples to the flock. . . . . . Likewise, ye younger, submit yourselves unto the elder. Yea, all of you be subject one to another, and be clothed with humility; for God resisteth the proud, and giveth grace to the humble."[a] No defence of a priestly dominion *could* be extracted from this passage; so perfectly has God's Spirit fenced it round on every side, and tempered one view by its opposite. But the words of Ignatius, taken as they stand, have a tendency to establish in the Christian Church tyranny in the rulers, and idolatry in the people; although I quite believe that if Ignatius had been questioned as to his meaning, he would earnestly have disclaimed the consequences of his language, and would have expressed himself more guardedly.

As to the general position, " that a fraction of any society cannot perform such acts as belong to the society itself," it is indisputably true. No individual, or small party of individuals, could be authorized to do any worldly act in the name of their society, unless they were commissioned by its acknowledged governors. A private man could not sell the church's property, nor give it away in

[a] [1 St. Peter, v. 1—5.]

alms; and so baptism, which is the admission of a new member into the church, requires to be performed by the church itself or with its sanction. And if it be essential to the Communion that it should be shared by all the members of the church, then it too becomes a public act, and requires of course the sanction of public authority. All this is true if we regard the church as a mere human society, and leads to no tyranny, because it wholly leaves untouched the great question, "What is to be done when the public authorities do not speak the sense of their society, but act wholly in opposition to it?" and merely goes upon the general and ordinary rule, "that the public authorities do represent their society, and are therefore justly considered to possess the exclusive power of acting in its name."

Yet, when we consider the tendencies of power to encroach more and more upon the rights of others, and the immense mischief of draining off as it were the whole vital activity of society into that small portion of it which exercises the supreme government, there is always a danger in making the individual ruler or rulers so completely the representatives of the body, as to sink the body itself into complete insignificance. What the fiction of the Lex Regia had made the emperors of Rome, that the words of Ignatius would make he bishops of the Christian Church; and when we hear him say, "wherever the bishop shall appear, there let the people be," we are reminded of a latter declaration of the most imperious despotism, "L'état, c'est moi." But most especially dangerous is such language in a religious society; for there despotism is apt soon to become priestcraft, and priestcraft is at once idolatry. And, therefore, our Lord and his Apostles, although they certainly did not wish to encourage turbulence and disobedience to lawful authority amongst Christians, yet have shown themselves no less careful in shutting the door against an excessive reverence for any human teacher or governor. And nothing can be more opposite than the impression likely to be produced by the words of Ignatius, "Follow all of you the bishop, as Jesus Christ followeth his Father: wherever the bishop shall appear, there let the people be; as, wheresoever Christ is, there is the Catholic Church," and especially that most rash expression, "He who does any thing without the knowledge of the bishop serves the Devil;" and by the words of Christ on the other side,—"Call no man your father upon earth; for one is your Father, who is in heaven:" and, "Be not ye called rabbi, for one is your master, even Christ, and all ye are brethren." ^a

Still, unguarded as is the language of Ignatius,

^a [St. Matthew, xxiii. 8, 9.]

and though it had a direct tendency to bring in priestcraft, and has been quoted repeatedly in support of the notion of a priesthood; yet it is only just to confess, that Ignatius himself appears to have had no such meaning. His words exaggerate unwisely the power and importance of Christian governors; they make them too universally and without exception the representatives of the church; but they acknowledge in them no priestly character. It is to avoid divisions that Ignatius will have no separate worship and no separate sacraments; he invests the bishop with the full character of the church, and so regards him as the appointed channel of God's gifts to the individual members of it; but it is to the body of the whole church, and not to an order of priests distinct from it, that he believes Christ's promises to have been given, and his authority conveyed. And although the two systems but too often lead practically to the same results, yet, in principle, they are widely different. A priesthood supposed to be of divine appointment is a hopeless evil; it requires nothing less than a new revelation to remove it. But the degree to which the governors of a society may be supposed to represent it, naturally varies according to times and circumstances. There are seasons of peril when a dictatorship affords the only means of safety; that is, when the rulers must wield the whole authority of society, and the rights and powers of the society must be merged in their persons altogether. But, in quieter times, society deputes far less of its authority, and it is most desirable that it should retain in itself no small portion of life and activity, lest it sink into utter helplessness. It may be that, in the days of Ignatius, the Church did wisely in committing to its rulers an almost absolute authority; it is most certain that it would act most unwisely if it were to do the same thing now.

Sect. 3. Epistle to the Magnesians.—In this epistle there occurs again much of the same sort of strong language which has been already noticed, as to the necessity of being closely united to the bishop and to the elders. But there is nothing connected with our present subject which seems to call for any separate notice.

Sect. 4. Epistle to the Trallians.—In this epistle we find the following passage, which I copy from the text of Mr. Jacobson's edition.

Δεῖ δὲ καὶ τοὺς διακόνους, ὄντας μυστηρίων Ἰησοῦ Χριστοῦ κατὰ πάντα τρόπον πᾶσιν ἀρέσκειν· οὐ γὰρ βρωμάτων καὶ ποτῶν εἰσιν διάκονοι, ἀλλ᾽ ἐκκλησίας Θεοῦ ὑπηρέται[a]. "Illos enim," so Vossius interprets, "non esse ministros esculentorum et poculentorum, sed ministros mysteriorum Dei, *sive sacramentorum.*" "The μυστήρια Ἰησοῦ Χριστοῦ are

[a] [Ad Trall. ii.]

the sacraments." This is with some a favourite doctrine, and we have seen already that they have not scrupled to ascribe it even to St. Paul, when he calls himself a steward of the mysteries of God. But here is the gradual growth of the corruption of Christianity. In St. Paul's language, "the mysteries of God" mean something quite different from the sacraments; in Ignatius, the expression probably includes the sacraments, but not as the principal part of the idea; in later writers, it would mean the sacraments principally, if not exclusively.

It may be observed, however, that the actual reading in Ignatius is not μυστηρίων but μυστήριον: the text runs thus in the single MS. now know to be in existence, τοὺς διακόνους, ὄντας μυστήριον Ἰησοῦ Χριστοῦ. But the old Latin translation, and the longer version of the epistles of Ignatius, agree in reading μυστηρίων, and it is also plain, from the corrupt state of the text in many places, that our single MS. is a very bad one. Arndt, of Ratzeburg, however, in an able paper on the genuineness of the epistles of Ignatius, in the 1st Number of the twelfth volume of the Theologische Studien und Kritiken, defends the reading μυστήριον, and interprets it in the sense of "likeness," "copy,"—referring to Polycarp's epistle to the Philippians, chap. v., where Christ is said to have been διάκονος πάντων. There seems therefore, on the whole, no reason to interfere with the actual reading of the MS. At any rate, if we adopt the reading μυστηρίων, the passage is not to be read as Mr. Jacobson has edited it, with a comma after διακόνους, but, τοὺς διακόνους ὄντας μυστηρίων, κ. τ. λ. "It befits those who are ministers of Christ's mysteries," &c. It now remains to be seen what Ignatius meant by διακόνους μυστηρίων Ἰησοῦ Χριστοῦ.

Now it may be true that Ignatius amongst the other μυστήρια of Christ would have included the sacraments: but the question is, whether the term express the sacraments either exclusively or principally. It cannot be too often repeated, that the whole question with which I am concerned regards the *prominence* of the sacraments in the scheme of Christianity, and by no means their *existence* in that scheme, which I am as ready to allow as any of those who esteem of them most highly. But did Ignatius regard the ministration of the sacraments as the principal part of the deacon's office, or did he include it merely as one out of many parts, and that not a prominent one? So that when he spoke of μυστήρια Χριστοῦ, he was thinking principally of other things than the sacraments, although, if he had been asked whether he meant the term to include the sacraments also, he might probably have answered in the affirmative?

a. The word μυστήριον occurs several times in the New Testament, but in no one place is there the least pretence for supposing that it so much as includes the sacraments, far less that it speaks of them principally. I have already noticed the palpable misinterpretation of St. Paul's words[a], where some have fancied that St. Paul meant to call himself a "dispenser of the sacraments." But with this exception, I do not know that any one has ventured, even wrongly, to ascribe this sense to the word. The confusion as to the meaning of the Latin word "sacramentum," which is the old translation of μυστήριον, in Ephesians v. 32. needs scarcely to be noticed; because neither does "sacramentum" in the language of the old Latin Christians mean what has been since technically called a "sacrament," nor is it applied to any rite or institution in which men can partake on earth, but to the wonderful incarnation of our Lord, in that he left his Father to join himself to our nature, and so to become one with us.

β. Ignatius himself twice uses the word μυστήριον in the scriptural sense; that is, "a truth or doctrine not discoverable by man but revealed to him by God." Thus the three truths, that Christ should have been born as a man, and born of a virgin, and that he should have died for us, are called by Ignatius "three mysteries," Ephes. 19; and Christ's

[a] [1 Corinth. iv. 1.]

life and death are again called "a mystery," Magnesians, 9; and he adds, "through this mystery we received our faith, and for the sake of this we wait patiently, that we may be found Christ's disciples." The probability is, therefore, that if Ignatius called the deacons "ministers of Christ's mysteries," he meant to call them "ministers of the great truths of Christianity," and not merely "ministers to distribute meat and drink to the poor in alms."

γ. Even in Cyprian's time the word "sacramentum," which was from the earliest period of the Church the corresponding Latin term to the Greek μυστήριον, is applied generally to the solemn and deep things of Christianity, without any especial reference to what are now called "sacraments." In Cyprian's 63rd letter, which contains a long argument on the necessity of using both water and wine in the cup at the Communion, the term "sacramentum" is applied, as we might expect, several times to various points in the institution of the Lord's Supper. So again, in the 72nd letter, we find it applied both to baptism and to the laying on of hands, or confirmation. But, in like manner, Cyprian speaks also of the many "sacramenta," "deep truths of God," which are contained in the Lord's Prayer[a]. So he speaks also of the "sacramentum Trinitatis," in his 73rd let-

[a] [De Oratione Dominicâ, p. 142; ed. Amstelod. 1691.]

ter; of the "sacramentum vitæ æternæ," in his Treatise on the Lord's Prayer, p. 151; of the "sacramentum unitatis," or mystery of the unity of the Church, and of the "sacramentum divinæ traditionis," letter 74th, where it means little more than "the sacredness of the lessons taught us by Christ and his Apostles." Thus it appears that, in the middle of the third century, and in the writings of a man sufficiently inclined to exalt the ordinances of the Church, the term sacramentum was not even yet exclusively applied to what have been since called sacraments.

Sect. 5. *Epistle to the Philadelphians.*—This epistle, besides various other passages, insisting on the necessity of uniting with the bishop, as in the other epistles, contains also the following:

Σπουδάσατε οὖν μιᾷ εὐχαριστίᾳ χρῆσθαι· μία γὰρ σὰρξ τοῦ Κυρίου ἡμῶν Ἰησοῦ Χριστοῦ καὶ ἓν ποτήριον εἰς ἕνωσιν τοῦ αἵματος αὐτοῦ· ἓν θυσιαστήριον ὡς εἷς ἐπίσκοπος, ἅμα τῷ πρεσβυτερίῳ καὶ διακόνοις τοῖς συνδούλοις μου, ἵνα ὃ ἐὰν πράσσητε κατὰ Θεὸν πράσσητε[a]. There is nothing here in what is said of the Communion deserving of remark, except the use of the word θυσιαστήριον. Did Ignatius mean to call the Communion table an altar, and the bishop who administered the Communion a priest sacrificing at the altar?

The answer is, that he did not: but that by the

[a] [Ad Philadelph. iv.]

term θυσιαστήριον he meant the Church of Christ, and the sacrifice to be offered on that altar was the sacrifice of prayer and praise, and of the bodies and souls of every Christian; and by combining together the words "one altar and one bishop," he meant that there should be only one Church and one government of it; not a multitude of separate bodies of Christians with their separate rulers: for that then the sacrifice of the Christian law would no longer be offered in unity.

That θυσιαστήριον in the early Christian writers signifies the Church of God, as St. Paul also calls the Church the ναός, or temple of God, may be shown from various instances. The earliest and best example of this is to be found in the New Testament itself, in the epistle to the Hebrews. There, in the 13th chapter, v. 10—15, we have the following remarkable words: Ἔχομεν θυσιαστήριον, ἐξ οὗ φαγεῖν οὐκ ἔχουσιν ἐξουσίαν οἱ τῇ σκηνῇ λατρεύοντες. κ. τ. λ. Where the argument runs thus: our sacrifice, as an atoning sacrifice must have been, was offered without the camp; that is, away from and out of the pale of the earthly Israel. We follow him without the camp also: our altar is no longer in the temple at Jerusalem, but without its precincts; it is where Christ was offered; that is virtually everywhere, where Christ's people are gathered together. There is their altar in the midst of their own company, and on that altar they offer up their sacrifices, now rendered acceptable through His atoning sacrifice, their spiritual sacrifice of prayer and praise and acts of charity. Of this altar the Jews have no right to eat; that is, as they would in the like case have no right to eat of the actual sacrifices offered on a literal altar which was quite distinct from their own temple, so they have no right to partake in the spiritual sacrifices of prayer and praise offered on the Christian altar, or in the spiritual bread of life, communion with Christ, which is there for ever present.

Thus also Polycarp, in his epistle to the Philippians, bids the widows of the Christian Church to remember that they are God's altar[a], and that every offering offered upon that altar must be without blemish[b]. That is, Christians themselves are God's spiritual altar, and their prayers, praises, and holy actions are the proper sacrifices to be offered upon it.

Thus also Ignatius himself, in his epistle to the Ephesians, says, "If a man be not within the altar, he fails to obtain the bread of God;"[c] and again, in

---

[a] So in the Apostol. Constitut. II. 26 ad fin., we find the same notion, αἱ χῆραι καὶ ὀρφανοὶ εἰς τύπον τοῦ θυσιαστηρίου λελογίσθωσαν ὑμῖν αἵ τε παρθένοι εἰς τύπον τοῦ θυμιατηρίου τετιμήσθωσαν, καὶ τοῦ θυμιάματος. Is this upon the notion that offerings were given for the widows, &c., and paid to them as on an altar?

[b] [Ad Philip. iv.] [c] [Ad Ephes. v.]

the epistle to the Trallians, "He that is within the altar, he is clean."[a] In the latter passage there follows immediately this explanation: "that is, he who does any thing apart from the bishop, and the company of elders, and the deacon, he is not clean in his conscience." And after the former passage the writer goes on, "For if the prayer of one or two persons has so great force, how much more is the force of the prayer of the bishop and of the whole Church?" It appears, therefore, from both these passages, that the altar is the Church of Christ, and that the sacrifices offered on it are prayers. And as it is said in the epistle to the Hebrews, that "the Jews have no right to eat of our altar," so Ignatius says, "that he who is without the Church cannot obtain the bread of God;" that is, as the shewbread under the law might be eaten only by the priests, so Christ, who is our Bread of life, is only to be enjoyed by those who are his priests, ministering at his altar, that is, by his people, who on the altar of his Church offer to him their prayers and themselves.

Sect. 6. *Epistle to Polycarp.*—In this epistle, I may notice the passage in which Christians proposing to marry are recommended to do it with the sanction and approbation of the bishop, in order that their marriage may be according to God, and not according to mere passion. This

[Ad Trall. vii.]

[I]

advice is remarkable, as it shows to what a length Ignatius carried his notions of unity, and what a Spartan discipline as to the merging the individual will in the will of the society, or of its representative, he would fain have introduced into the Christian Church. Regarding the bishops of the several churches as men eminently fitted to bring their people to the purest state of Christian perfection, and considering that amongst their people, their subjects I might almost call them, there existed the greatest varieties of wild opinion and licentious practice, he saw no other remedy than to invest the rulers of the Church with absolute authority. Hence, he not only wished to unite in their persons every power of government, and to subject to their absolute control every thing that might be called a public or social act of the Church as a body; as when he would have no Communion celebrated without the bishop's authority; but he would even give them dominion over acts most strictly belonging to the individual Christian; even for marriage he would require their sanction, as being the fathers of the Christian family: they were to judge whether the proposed union was entered upon in a Christian spirit, or whether it was desired from mere youthful passion. Now this subjection of the individual to the society, even in the most private relations of domestic life, was very agreeable to the spirit of many of the ideal commonwealths of the Greek philosophy: and, in the famous constitution of Sparta, it had been actually established in practice. Much was to be said on its behalf, by those especially who were most aware of the evils of the opposite extreme, of leaving the individual will wholly uncontrolled, except if it should attempt to offer a direct injury to another. Nor can we doubt that Ignatius recommended pure despotism as sincerely and as conscientiously as ever men of different views and under different circumstances have protested against it. But instead of seeing in the letters of Ignatius a strong display of views which have been often entertained by wise and good men, and which in this particular case were more than ordinarily justified by the peculiar circumstances of the Church, men have sought to find in him a perpetual law of Church government, and have taken his most vehement expressions as an authoritative definition of the powers which ought to be always exercised by the rulers of the Christian society. Nor is this all; but as persons who have been capable of so misusing him were not likely to have very clear notions of government and the questions connected with it, so it has happened that confounding different times and usages, and being the slaves of a name, they have transferred what Ignatius says of the necessity of an absolute government in the hands of the bishop, to the later system of the mystical power of the priesthood; and where he would acknowledge nothing as an act of the church which was not done by the authority of the bishop, they have quoted him as sanctioning their doctrine of the necessity of a priestly consecration of the elements to the sacramental virtue of the Lord's Supper: where he would have the bishop's consent obtained for all marriages, that they might be such as a Christian ought to contract, he has been quoted as enforcing the necessity of the priestly benediction to give to the rite of marriage any validity.[a]

Here then we close our present inquiry: but one or two points seem naturally to arise from it, and with some notice of these I will conclude this chapter.

1st. We do not find in these early Christian writers the doctrine of the priesthood and sa-

[a] "Hinc clare patet," says Smith. "nuptias non fuisse habitas justas et legitimas absque sententiâ episcopi, *et benedictione sacerdotali*, in primis Christianismi seculis." Smith is confounding two ideas perfectly distinct, one of which Ignatius had, while of the other not the slightest trace is to be found in him. He did wish that the bishop should have the power of a father over the whole church, that his consent should be obtained before any Christian could marry. This is a power of government, and this he undoubtedly wished to give to the bishop of every church. But to require a priestly blessing in order to hallow the rite of marriage is a very different notion, and one of which Ignatius says nothing whatever.

craments which was afterwards prevalent in the Church; but we find language which will sufficiently account for the subsequent introduction of that doctrine; whereas the Scriptures not only do not contain it, but absolutely repel it: between them and it there is a great gulf fixed, over which no art of man can cast a bridge.

2nd. A full consideration of this language in the early uncanonical writers, will lead to three conclusions. While, in the first place, it marks the wide distinction between them and the Scripture, and should lead us to thank God that the scriptural writers were so secured by his Spirit, not from error only, but from such unguarded and one-sided language, if I may so speak, as might readily become the occasion of error; we shall, in the second place, be spared the pain of believing that Christianity was grossly corrupted in the very next generation after the Apostles by the men who professed themselves to be the Apostles' true followers. We shall rather have reason to believe that their language, taken in their own meaning, and as applied to the circumstances of the Church in their own times, was substantially true. We shall be able to sympathize with Ignatius in his earnest desire to keep the Church in unity with its bishops, and with Clement in his sense of the value of their Apostolical succession; we shall readily confess that to this unity, and this real

Apostolical succession of the early bishops, we owe the general acknowledgment of the authority of the Apostles and of their writings;—we owe it, in fact, that our Christianity at this day is that of St. John, and not of Cerinthus; of St. Paul, and not of his Judaizing adversaries. And thirdly, comparing these early Christian writers with the Scriptures on the one hand, and with the later Church system on the other, as developed in the forged Apostolical constitutions, we shall be able to trace three stages through which Christianity passed, and which, indeed, exhibit what may be called the law of decay in all institutions, whether administered by men only, or devised by them as well as administered. The first and perfect state exhibits the spirit of the institution not absolutely without all forms, for that is impossible, but regarding them as things wholly subordinate, indifferent in themselves, and therefore deriving their value from particular times and circumstances; and as such particular times are not yet come, the spirit of the institution is as yet wholly independent of them; it uses their ministry, but in no way depends upon their aid. Then comes the second stage, when from particular circumstances the existence of the spirit of the institution depends on the adherence to particular outward regulations. The men of this generation insist, as well they may, on the necessity of these forms, for without them the spirit would be lost. And because others profess to honour the spirit no less than they do, there-fore they are obliged to make the forms rather than the spirit their peculiar rallying word. Around and for these forms is the stress of battle: but their defenders well know that they are but the husk in which the seed of life is sheltered; that they are but precious for the sake of the seed which they contain, and to the future growth of which they, under the inclemencies of the actual season, are an indispensable condition.

Then the storm passes away, and the precious seed, safely sheltered within its husk, has escaped destruction. The forms have done their appointed work, and, like the best of mortal instruments, their end should be, that after having served their own generation by the will of God, they should fall asleep and see corruption. But in the third stage men cannot understand this law. Their fathers clung to certain forms to the death; they said—and said truly—that unless these were preserved, the spirit would perish. The sons repeat their fathers' words, although in their mouths they are become a lie. Their fathers insisted on the forms even more earnestly than on the spirit, because in their day the forms were peculiarly threatened. But now the forms are securely established, and the great enemy who strove to destroy them whilst they protected the seed of life, is now as ready to uphold them, because they may become the means of stifling it. But the sons, unheeding of this change, still insist mainly on the importance of the forms, and seeing these triumphant, they rejoice, and think that the victory is won, just at the moment when a new battle is to be fought, and the forms oppress the seed instead of protecting it. Still they uphold the form, for that is a visible object of worship, and they teach their children to do the same. Age after age the same language is repeated, whilst age after age its falsehood is becoming more flagrant; and still it is said, "We are treading in the steps of our fathers from the very beginning; even at the very first these forms were held to be essential." So when the husk cracks, and would fain fall to pieces by the natural swelling of the seed within, a foolish zeal labours to hold it together: they who would deliver the seed, are taxed with longing to destroy it; they who are smothering it, pretend that they are treading in the good old ways, and that the husk was, is, and ever will be essential. And this happens because men regard the form and not the substance; because they think that to echo the language of their forefathers is to be the faithful imitators of their spirit; because they are blind to the lessons which all nature teaches them, and would for ever keep the egg-shell unbroken, and the sheath of the leaf unburst, not seeing that the wisdom of winter is the folly of spring.

So it has been with the unity of the Church under its bishops, and with their apostolical succession. In the second stage of the Church, these were really essential to the protection of Christian truth: in its third stage, through many generations they have been a mere empty name, powerless to preserve or to increase the spirit of Christianity, but often only too powerful in stifling and in corrupting it.

CHAPTER IV.

In the inquiry which has been pursued through the last two chapters, we have seen that the doctrine of the priesthood is repelled by the Scriptures, and not acknowledged by the earliest uncanonical Christians. The first of these results ought to be abundantly sufficient for our practice: the doctrine which the Scripture not only does not teach, but which it virtually condemns, must be inconsistent with Christianity. The second result, although not needed practically, is yet on two accounts interesting. It is satisfactory to find that the Church in the very first century had not grossly corrupted Christian truth. It is also satisfactory to find in the peculiar circumstances and language of these early writers, an explanation, and something of a palliation for the grievous errors of the subsequent age. Had any generation of Christians fallen at once from the perfect spirit of Scriptural truth into the doctrine of the priesthood, it would have seemed hardly less than apostasy from the faith; but Ignatius and his contemporaries exhibit the Church in a sort of transition state, which, although not one of error, yet rendered the actual errors of the following period more excusable. We now proceed to see how the errors themselves came in;

how government was converted into priesthood, and how Judaism, driven from its own ceremonies, and obliged to abandon circumcision and the distinction of clean and unclean meats, took possession of the Christian sacraments, and held with effect under their names the very same mischievous doctrines which, when connected with the names of Jewish ceremonies, the Church had been so earnestly warned to avoid. So what took place with regard to the sacraments, was the exact converse of what happened with respect to Apostolical succession; each instance equally confirming the truth, that men are ruled by names and not by things. On the one hand, the benefits of a real Apostolical succession were supposed to be retained, because there was still an Apostolical succession nominally: on the other hand, men thought that they were safe from Judaism, because they put the word baptism in the place of circumcision, and talked of the mystic virtue of the elements in the Communion, instead of the purifying nature of clean meats, and the defiling character of such as were unclean.

Let us now see in what respects the Church, early in the second century, was ready to slide into the doctrine of a priesthood, with all its accompanying corruptions of Christian truth.

The beginning of the second century found the Church under the government of bishops, many of whom had derived their appointment from the Apostles themselves, at only one or two removes; that is to say, they had been chosen by men who had themselves been chosen by an Apostle, or by persons such as Timotheus, in whom an Apostle had entertained full confidence. They were engaged in an arduous struggle not only against heathenism, but against various monstrous forms of error which claimed to themselves the name of Christianity; and, as happens naturally in such times of danger, they drew to themselves more and more, not through ambition, but by the necessity of the case, the whole power of the Christian society. They were the representatives of the Church, and without them the Church had no existence; those were not the prayers of the Church, that was not her Communion, which the bishop did not either preside at or sanction. Here, then, was a government of a religious society, whose sanction was considered necessary to the religious acts of that society, and which grounded its claim to obedience mainly on the fact that it derived its authority all but immediately from the Apostles, and so might be supposed to represent them faithfully. We see here at once two facts, which, with a very little corruption, might become two of the most essential elements of a priesthood; we see the germ of the necessity of a priestly consecration of the elements in the sacraments, and of the transmission of the priestly character by a sort of elective succession.

Now, if it had pleased God that the Church at this period should have become a sovereign society, as it did two centuries later, it might have been more easy to prevent the government of the bishops from being confounded with the notion of a priesthood. Had they been able, that is, to exercise the full powers of government, to control society in the last resort, and to exercise jurisdiction over life and property, the largeness and outward greatness of their functions would have so satisfied men's minds, that none would have sought for them any higher or nobler office than that which they were manifestly seen to exercise. But government in a subordinate society, and divested consequently of its sovereign character, is of necessity far less imposing. As a government, it is wholly eclipsed, to the vulgar eye at any rate, by that greater government of general or sovereign society, to which it must be itself subject. Considered as a ruler, the bishop of a Christian church appeared a far less important person than the Proconsul of a province; the most numerous synod was as nothing when compared with the sovereign of the Empire. Yet there was in the Church a greatness more than the Empire could boast of; there was a sense in which its bishops were greater than Cæsar. For a time this was even outward and tangible; so long as the Apostles possessed and conferred those extraordinary gifts of the Holy Spirit, which no wealth of man could purchase, nor power compel. When these were withdrawn, the real greatness still remained, but it was such as common minds can with difficulty appreciate. The moral elevation conferred by truth and holiness; the willing obedience of good men; the task of guiding a society whose members spiritually considered were privileged far above the rest of mankind, to be as it were the salt of the very salt of the earth itself; these were points of greatness most real and most exalted. But the mind of man, disappointed of what is outward and sensible, turns not to what is spiritual, but to what is mystical; unsatisfied with the real excellence of the office of a Christian Bishop, it coveted the mystical and false dominion of a priest.

According to Christ's ordinance, the rulers of the church were distinguished above their brethren in all that may be called the human relations of the Christian society; they had authority both to teach and to govern. The one only occasion on which this distinction was to cease, was when the church as a body came into direct relation with God and Christ; that is to say, in its public prayers, and in the Holy Communion. Rulers and teachers cease to be distinguished from the people, exactly in those acts in which the priest's distinction is greatest. Others may teach, and others may govern; for these are human relations: but in direct relation with God, the priest's mediation is wanted; he must pray for the people, and their communion with God can only be carried on through him. But as prayer and the Holy Communion were the church's most solemn acts, as a body, if its rulers here were on a level with other Christians, it seemed to lessen the dignity of their office. It was not enough that the presence or sanction of the bishop was required to render the Christian supper a true Communion of the church; nor that, in the celebration of it, the bread and wine were, to prevent confusion, distributed by the principal members of the society, either by the bishop himself or by the elders. The priestly mystical power, which seemed so much greater than the mere government of a subordinate or municipal society, was not here to be found. Another step was to be taken, not only that the bishop's authority as head of the church should be required in order to invest any meeting of Christians with the public character of the church, but that religiously the church itself could not communicate with Christ without the mediation, not of the bishop alone, but of the bishop or some one of his presbyters, all of whom were to possess equally with him this mediatorial character. Nor was it to be a mere matter of order that the bread and wine were distributed by those who presided at the meeting to the several communicants, after the usual form of thanksgiving before meat had been uttered; but from this distribution and this form of thanksgiving they were to derive their sacramental virtue, and having been before mere common bread and wine, they became immediately, through the virtue of the words so uttered, and of the priestly character of him who uttered them, changed into the body and blood of Christ. It could not but follow from this, that the Communion should be represented as an actual, not a spiritual sacrifice, in which there was a visible offering made, and which therefore required a priest.

But one of the oldest representations now extant, of the celebration of the Communion in the ancient Church, seems in a remarkable manner to avoid these corruptions. I allude to the famous fragment of Irenæus, first published by Pfaff, from a MS. in the library of Turin, and given in the Benedictine edition of the works of Irenæus, Venice, 1734. In this famous passage, Irenæus contrasts the spiritual sacrifices of Christianity with the carnal sacrifices of the Jewish law. He divides the Christian sacrifices into two kinds; those of prayer and thanksgiving, and those which consist in the offering up of ourselves to God, to do him service. "Wherefore," says he, "the offering also of the Eucharist is not carnal but spiritual, and thereby it is clean (καθαρά). For we offer to God the bread, and the cup of blessing, rendering thanks to him, for that he has bidden the earth to bring forth these fruits for our nourishment. And here, having completed our offering, we call upon the Holy Spirit, that he may render (ἀποφήνῃ) this sacrifice to be, both the bread the body of Christ, and the cup the blood of Christ, that they who have partaken of these symbols (ἀντιτύπων) may obtain forgiveness of their sins, and life eternal. They, then, who bring these offerings in remembrance of the Lord, do not join themselves to the ordinances of the Jews, but worshipping (λειτουργοῦντες) spiritually, shall be called the children of wisdom."

Now this most remarkable passage exhibits in a surprising completeness that notion of the Communion which has been given in the first chapter of this work. The sacrifices or offerings of Christians must be spiritual, for we must worship God in spirit and in truth; and the offering of the Eucharist is *therefore* a clean and accepted offering, because it is *spiritual*. How then is the Eucharist a *spiritual* sacrifice? Not because of the offering of bread and wine, but because of spiritual acts accompanying or following that offering; the acts, namely, of thanksgiving and prayer. Of thanks-

[K]

giving, when we thank God while offering the bread and wine before Him, that He has given us these things for our bodily sustenance: of prayer, when, after having completed the offering, and partaken of the bread and wine, we pray to God the Holy Spirit, that He will make that temporal food also a spiritual food; and that as bread and wine support our bodies, so, whilst in eating that bread and drinking that wine we remember Christ's body and Christ's blood, His body and blood may be the redemption and the strengthening of our souls to everlasting life. Thus, the bread that perisheth is changed by the Holy Spirit into the bread of life; having eaten bodily for our bodily good, the Holy Spirit guides us to eat spiritually for our spiritual good. But the soul feeds itself not with the mouth and teeth, but by thoughts and love. To eat spiritually, is to assimilate an object to our spirits by drawing it to them by thought, and embracing it by love. He, therefore, who eateth Christ shall live by him; because, by believing in Christ and loving him, he takes Christ into his spirit, and his nature becomes assimilated to that of Christ, and so he lives and must live for ever. Truly, therefore, says Irenæus, that they who offer the bread and wine to God, in remembrance of the Lord Jesus, that is, who, after having partaken of their bodily food, and therefore, *every day*, do pray to the Holy

Spirit that their souls may feed upon Christ no less as their spiritual food; they by that prayer convert what else would be a formal and Jewish sacrifice into one that is Christian and spiritual. Their service to God (Λειτουργία) is a spiritual service, and they who so serve Him have no fellowship with the ordinances of the Jews, but shall be called the children of wisdom.

But observe that here, in this description of the Christian Communion, there is no mention of a priest's words of consecration changing the bread and wine *beforehand* into the body and blood of Christ; and so giving occasion to all manner of superstitions and profaneness. The bread and wine are received with thanksgiving, *as bread and wine*, as fruits of the earth, which God our Creator has commanded the earth to yield for our bodily support. Then, *after they have been received*, comes, not a form of consecration by an earthly priest, but a prayer to God the Holy Spirit, to Him who communes with us only as spirits, dealing not with our natural life, but with our spiritual; that He may render to each of us the bodily and outward offering a spiritual and inward offering; that by eating bread and drinking wine, not simply as fruits of the earth, but in remembrance of Christ's death, our spirits may feed upon Christ himself, in all his manifold relations to us, and so be strengthened by him and become like to him more and more. In other words, we pray to the Holy Spirit to keep alive in us daily our spiritual appetites and powers, that they may desire Christ and receive him into themselves, as naturally—naturally, I mean, according to our renewed nature—as the healthy body according to its nature desires and digests its bodily food.

* * * * *

FRAGMENTS

ON

CHURCH AND STATE:

WRITTEN IN 1827—1840,

AND PUBLISHED AS

APPENDICES TO THE FIRST EDITION

OF THE

FRAGMENT ON THE CHURCH.

BY

THOMAS ARNOLD, D.D.,

LATE HEAD MASTER OF RUGBY SCHOOL.

LONDON:
B. FELLOWES, LUDGATE STREET.

1845.

LONDON:
GEORGE WOODFALL AND SON,
ANGEL COURT, SKINNER STREET.

PREFACE.

THE following sketches and fragments, on mature consideration, were found to form so natural an accompaniment to the "Fragment on the Church," already published, that it has been thought best, even at the risk of some temporary inconvenience, to give them to the public in a form which will facilitate this arrangement, rather than to place them, as was originally proposed, in the forthcoming volume of Miscellaneous works.

They are, as will be seen, earlier approaches to the same subject as that which the Author finally treated in the Fragment to which they are here appended; and, though with some unavoidable repetition, give severally the different parts of the subject which he was led to treat at one time more fully than at another, according as he was led to enter upon it from different points of view.

APPENDIX I.

PLAN OF A WORK, "CHRISTIAN POLITICS," IN 1827.

Of the end of man's existence.
Of the end of political society.
How far these ends have been hitherto answered.
Of Christianity as the means of effecting these ends, and of the grounds of its authority.
Of the manner in which the end of individual existence modifies the end of political existence.
How political happiness is best promoted by not being the principal end of man in society.
How political happiness is to be effected.
    § 1. Of physical or external happiness.
    § 2. Of Moral or internal happiness.
  1. Physical happiness, affected by—
    § 1. The state of personal liberty and safety.
    § 2. The amount and distribution of national wealth.
  2. Moral happiness, affected by—
    § 1. The state of political liberty.
    § 2. The amount of intellectual improvement.
    § 3. The amount of spiritual improvement.

Of education as the means of obtaining moral happiness.
    § 1. Of political education.
    § 2. Of intellectual education.
    § 3. Of spiritual education.

This was the sketch of a work alluded to in Sermons, vol. i. p. 88, and in two letters in 1827:

"What say you to a work on πολιτικὴ, in the old Greek sense of the word, in which I should try to apply the principles of the Gospel to the legislation and administration of a state. It would begin with a simple statement of the τέλος of man according to Christianity, and then would go on to show how the knowledge of this τέλος would affect all our views of national wealth, and the whole question of political economy; and also our practice with regard to wars, oaths, and various other relics of the στοιχεῖα τοῦ κόσμου."

"I have long had in my mind a work on Christian Politics, or the application of the Gospel to the state of man as a citizen, in which the whole question of a religious establishment and of the education proper for Christian members of a Christian commonwealth would naturally find a place. It would embrace also an historical sketch of the pretended conversion of the kingdoms of the world to the kingdom of Christ in the fourth and fifth centuries, which I look upon as one of the greatest *tours d'adresse* that Satan ever played, except his invention of Popery. I mean that by inducing kings and nations to conform nominally to Christianity, and thus to get into their hands the direction of Christian society, he has in a great measure succeeded in keeping out the peculiar principles of that society from any extended sphere of operation, and in ensuring the ascendancy of his own. One real conversion there seems to have been, that of the Anglo-Saxons; but that he soon succeeded in corrupting; and at the Norman Conquest we had little I suppose to lose even from the more direct introduction of Popery and worldly religion which came in with the Conqueror."[a]

This work was never carried out, and would, in some points, have differed from the later fragments on the same subject. In illustration of the point of view from which the question was here approached, is given the following extract from an unpublished Preface to a volume of Sermons in 1829.

" Whether in any case the union, as it is called, of Church and State was desirable is another question; but wherever that union does exist, then the Gospel is directly brought into contact with political institutions and measures, and is required to apply its purifying influence to the conduct of governments no less than to that of private individuals. Of direct precepts indeed, addressed by Christ and His Apostles to kings and statesmen, there must necessarily be none ; but of principles eminently applicable to the government of nations, of the spirit which should influence all public measures, he must be greatly ignorant of the Gospel who cannot find innumerable instances. Under other circumstances, the Christian minister may perhaps be allowed to confine himself to the care of the poor and ignorant: but the clergy of a national church are directly called upon to Christianize the nation: not only to inculcate the private virtues of the Gospel,— but its pure and holy principles in their full extent; those divine laws, of which it may indeed be said, that their ' voice is the harmony of the world.' And this duty the Church of England has eminently neglected;

[a] Life and Correspondence, vol. i. pp. 52, 3. 4th edit.

and to the servility of its political principles alone, the neglect is chargeable. Did it become a Christian Church to make no other official declaration of its sentiments concerning war, than by saying that Christian men might lawfully engage in it; to say nothing of capital punishments with the bloody executions of Henry the Eighth's reign, so fresh in memory, but that they might be lawfully inflicted on Christian men for heinous and grievous offences? Or, because the Anabaptists, as the Waldenses had done before them, had gone so far as to refuse to take an oath at all, did it become a Christian Church to confine the principle of our Lord's prohibition to 'vain and rash swearing' only, and to leave the practice of legal oaths, not as a relic of an unchristian state of society, which we to our shame were not sufficiently advanced in the Gospel to renounce, but as a thing absolutely good now, as formerly under the dispensation of the Jews? Will it be asked what evil has arisen from this neglect of duty? I answer, that the evil is to be seen in the unchristian principles and practice of our rulers, and of all public men considered as such from the Reformation down to this very hour. Or was it vain to expect that any exertions of the Church could have made this kingdom in reality, as well as in name, a kingdom of Christ? Vain, perhaps, it would be to expect a result so glorious; yet, surely much was practicable, and it has been noted as a mark of folly for more than two thousand years, not to know 'how much the half is more valuable than the whole.' Nay experience itself has shown, what can be done even with far inferior means, when there is an active and Christian zeal at work. What is the present feeling in this country with regard to the Slave Trade, and how far must we look back to trace it to its origin? Its very birth is almost within the recollection of men now living; its strength and universality falls within my own. And has the Church of England as a body been forward in exciting this feeling; most of all is to the High Church divines that we are indebted for it? The moving spring must be sought elsewhere, and the comparatively powerless sect of the Quakers has done more to imbue the nation with a Christian sense of the wickedness of stealing men to sell them as slaves, than was ever attempted by the vast influence of the Established Church:—because the Church of England is so dependent on the State, (more by the feelings of its members than by its legal constitution,) that instead of striving to grow up into a true branch of Christ's glorious Church, perfect even after the infinite perfection of its Head, its notions of excellence have been lowered by the actual constitution in Church and State, by idle language about the doctrines of the Reformers, and the excellence of the British constitution. As if the sixteenth and seventeenth centuries, scarcely waking as they were from the accumulated moral ignorance and insensibility of thirty generations, could offer any thing to satisfy our aspirations after Christian excellence; as if the consummated work of the Spirit of God were to be found in the dregs of the Papal and Feudal institutions!

" This great neglect of its highest duties is not peculiar, certainly, to the Church of England; it is the besetting sin of every church establishment, from the nominal conversion of the Roman emperors, down to this very hour. No doubt the influence of Christianity has made itself felt in all those countries which have professed it; but ought not its effects to have been far more perceptible than they are, now that nearly eighteen hundred years have elapsed since the kingdom of God was first proclaimed? Is it, in fact, the kingdom of God in which we are living? Are we at this hour living under the law, or under grace? I may be told that it is chimerical to expect such a state of things as the Apostles, in their earlier Epistles at least, seem to have anticipated; that the splendid pictures of older prophecy must not be interpreted too literally; that when the Angels welcomed the birth of the Prince of Peace, with announcing peace on earth, they but alluded to the fact of the comparative tranquillity of the Roman world at that time, and augured nothing of the future state of the world. There are some prophecies which fulfil themselves, and some opinions, also, which insure their own perpetual truth; and amongst these, none is more memorable than that favourite tenet of public and practical men, as they call themselves, that mankind will always be much the same as they now are, and that to hope for any great improvement among them is visionary; and, suiting to these low and unbelieving principles a practice consistently unworthy, they have kept the world in its present state of badness. They talk of experience, but it is all against them; for all the good that has been done in the world, has been done by acting in direct opposition to their theory; while all the evil that exists is its proper and natural fruit. Superstition has been called in to aid this corrupt doctrine; and men have been so blinded by their reverence for antiquity, as to substitute the primitive Church, such as it actually existed, in the place of that perfect Church which never has yet existed, but which Christ designed as our standard of excellence, and the object of all our endeavours to accomplish; and, by a cunning mixture of truth with falsehood, and assuming a language apparently full of reverence for the Scriptures, and indignant at what it calls a profane disrespect to them, they have laboured to make us rest contented with our present state, by saying that nothing new can now be discovered in Christianity, and that we have nothing to do but to follow those primitive ages, which, as being nearer in time to the Apostles, must have been better acquainted with their doctrines than we can pretend to be. There is enough of truth in this language, and enough semblance of piety, to make it more extensively mischievous. The tenets which it is designed to combat have been carried, certainly, to a length no less injurious; and ordinary and unfair minds cannot be expected, perhaps, to separate truth from error when they are mixed together in the opinions of their adversaries. What causes produced the unchristian doctrines of many of the divines of modern Germany, Mr. Pusey's excellent work on that subject has sufficiently shown us; and they are such as well deserve the notice of our High Church divines. When the orthodox theologians, as they were called, had lost sight of the very purpose for which the Gospel was given,—the restoration of our moral nature from its state of corrupt principles and practice, and the raising it into a capacity of enjoying everlasting communion with God,—they, of all men, ought to have judged lightly of the error of the Rationalists in discarding what their own representations had already deprived of all its value. For so long as the great doctrines of Christianity are used as the Scripture uses them,—for the purpose of giving us particular motives and particular feelings,—so long they are, indeed, the very bread of life, and he who eateth of that bread shall live for ever. But when dissevered from their moral influence, when represented as awful mysteries, as objects of knowledge or of historical faith, they become like the manna of old; when no longer used as God designed them to be used, they are of all things the most worthless.

"The error then of the German Rationalists was great, but less mischievous than that of the orthodox divines who had preceded them. I say less mischievous,—because their attack on the form of Christianity created at once a general alarm, and is at this moment producing a most beneficial reaction; whereas the deadening of the spirit of the Gospel was an evil which went on surely and secretly, awakening no suspicion, and spreading every year a more deep and deadly slumber. Our divines are certainly far from meriting the censure which must be passed on those of the orthodox school in Germany: yet in their fondness for ecclesiastical rather than scriptural terms; in looking at the scripture through the unworthy medium of the Fathers and the Reformers, instead of applying the added experience of each successive age to develope its riches in their full perfection, they have helped to stunt the growth of Christ's Church, and have caused Christians in general still to linger round those elements of Gospel truth which the author of the Epistle to the Hebrews expected Christians even in this day to have left behind them in their progress. For though it be most true, that there is no new fact in Christianity to be learnt, and nothing to be discovered which does not really follow from those principles contained in the writings of the Apostles; yet it is not true that those principles have been even yet fully developed, or made to yield all that abundance of Divine wisdom which is actually to be drawn from them. The promise of the Spirit of Truth to abide for ever with his Church, implies surely that clearer views of truth should be continually vouchsafed to us; and if the work were indeed fully complete when the Apostles entered into their rest, what need was there for the Spirit of Wisdom, as well as of Love, to be ever present even unto the end of the world. They, however, must think very strangely of this Eternal Comforter and Guide, who imagine His influence to be communicated without any outward means, as an inspiration vouchsafed to a passive and often a careless recipient. " He shall glorify me," said Christ, "for He shall take of mine and shall show it unto you." It is by the study of the great principles of all goodness and all wisdom contained in the Christian Scriptures, that we are fashioned after our imperfect measure to goodness and wisdom also. But for this study to be profitable in the highest possible degree, we see in practice that large experience, that a spirit rising above the influence of its age, and a pure love of excellence, combined with a clear and manly understanding, are all necessary. How is it conceivable that the innocence of pious frauds could have been so long maintained by sincere Christians in the earliest ages, and the duty of religious persecution so strenuously insisted on at a later period, if something more than the mere possession, or even than the mere devout reading of the Scriptures were not necessary in order to extract from them their full virtue. It is not only for the critical knowledge of the New Testament that study and some intellectual exertion are requisite; but much more must the understanding work vigorously and freely, and be unfettered by the corrupt notions of the world, before it can develope the moral excellence of the Gospel. We are shocked at those persons who cannot perceive that the whole spirit and principles of Christianity are a sufficient condemnation of suicide, although there be no express words which say, ' Thou shall not kill thyself.' Yet, it is something of the same blindness which has made them declare that the New Testament does not condemn the existing civil institutions of mankind, when most of those institutions are founded on principles wholly inconsistent with Christian purity, and lead in practice to various forms of corruption, error, and injustice. It is the work of the Spirit of wisdom, so to enlighten the sincere lover of goodness as to enable him gradually to rise in his views of perfection: to forget those things which are behind, and to press forward to those which are before: to follow up the principles of the Scripture to all their conclusions, which the ignorant or the dishonest reader has never arrived at; to strive for himself individually, and for that Christian nation to which he belongs, that they shall stir up the gift given unto them, abounding more and more in knowledge and in all judgment; till every relic of our evil nature be destroyed in principle, at least, if not in practice, and every thought and word be brought into the obedience of Christ, even if our deeds should still revolt from Him.

" The ordinary answer to all this, if answer it may be called, consists in mere random charges of enthusiasm and impracticability;—such doctrines sound well in theory, but will not do, we are told, in practice. But to what is it that all the improvements in the world are to be ascribed, but to these high and aspiring principles; to what is every corruption, every folly, every existing wickedness imputable, but to the low notions of those who call themselves practical, and who, forming their models from their own practice, and that of others like them, ensure the perpetual grovelling of themselves, and all who listen to them in the degradation of their actual vileness? That blessed Gospel, which these practical men pretend to reverence, is full of what they must consider the wildest theories; and the heights to which it strives to raise us, and from which we are ever shrinking backwards, from a love of our native depths, are indeed unattainable to all who resolve to think them so. But read the Prophets, read the Apostles, read the words of the Lord of both Prophets and Apostles, and say if there is any limit to that perfection in virtue and in happiness which they call upon the Church of God to thirst after. Let St. Paul speak for all the rest." . . . . . .

[The MS. is here broken off. The passage on which the author was about to dwell, seems to have been Eph. iv. 11—13, to which, with that already quoted from Heb. vi. 1, he used frequently to refer in illustration of the views here set forth. "What is the progress spoken of?" he used to say. "It is in the application of Christianity to human things—the progress in this is as endless as the progress from our imperfection to perfection can be."]

APPENDIX II.

PLAN OF A WORK ON "CHRISTIAN POLITICS," DRAWN UP IN OCTOBER, 1833.

EVILS OF DISSENT:—
    Politically, as dividing the people into parties.
    Morally, as dividing and weakening the efforts of good men, to improve the moral state of society.

CAUSES OF DISSENT:—
    General Causes: The varieties of the human mind, and the inveterate mistaking of the nature of Christian union.
    Particular causes in England: The imperfect constitution of the Established Church, and political differences.

PROPOSED REMEDIES:—
    The abolition of a Church Establishment altogether.
    The giving all civil rights to Dissenters, and confirming and increasing their separation from the Establishment.

THE TRUE REMEDY:—
    An enlarged constitution of the Christian Church of England, which is the State of England.

APPENDIX II.

OBJECTIONS TO THIS REMEDY:—
> Popular and utilitarian: That the State as such has nothing to do with religion.
> Superstitious and fanatical: That the Church is distinct from the State and independent of it, having a divinely appointed government of its own.

OBJECTIONS ANSWERED:—
> The State in a Christian country is the Church, and therefore has much to do with religion.
> The Church, as such, has no divinely appointed government.
> The true view of Church and State obviates many evils which have arisen from the confused notion of them; evils—on the one hand of laxity and on the other of persecution.
> Confused notions about excommunication and spiritual power.
> Confused notions of Christian unity and faith.

PRACTICAL OBJECTIONS:—
> The actual feelings of the Church party and of the Dissenters.

GENERAL BEARING OF SUCH A TRUE CHURCH OF ENGLAND ON THE NATIONAL WELFARE:—*e. g.*,
> On national education; on the condition of the poorer classes in manufacturing districts; on the morals and knowledge of all classes of the community.

[The foregoing sketch was drawn up in the autumn of 1833 in pursuance of an intention then expressed of attempting a "Christian Aristotle's Politics," which should unfold at length his views on Church and State. The two following fragments were in part executions of the same design, though not exactly of the same plan.]

(A.) ON THE ENDS OF THE CHURCH.

Written apparently in the Summer of 1833.

CHAPTER I.

No good man can doubt, when he looks at the actual condition of this country, that the principal evils which actually oppress it, and which threaten it for the future in a still greater degree, are neither physical nor political, in the common sense of the word, but moral evils. Wide as may be the differences of opinion with respect to the remedy for these evils, or even their cause, yet their amount, and the probability of their increase, will hardly be disputed. In fact, the physical and political evils which exist are owing chiefly to the moral evils; and would be removed, not wholly, perhaps, but in great part, if the state of the country were improved morally. Those who fear the growing power of the poorer classes, fear it because they think that these classes are morally ignorant, and therefore are not fit to exercise power; those who dread the ascendancy of the aristocracy, and the consequent maintenance of all abuses, believe that the richer classes are morally ignorant also, and disposed to turn their advantages to their own benefit, and not to that of the whole community. The very distress of the poor is attributed by some to their own improvidence and carelessness; by others, to the neglect and selfishness of the rich In short, whatever evil is most apprehended by any party, is generally ascribed to some moral defect in the opposite party; and if this defect could be abated, the danger, to say the least, would be felt to be greatly diminished.

But the benefits which might arise from the general acknowledgment of the real evil of our condition are generally frustrated by the belief that the evil is incurable. For physical and political evils men are prompt enough in devising remedies: they understand, also, that where individual efforts would be powerless to remove them, combination and the mechanism of society may undertake the task with success. But moral evil is left hopelessly to itself, or, at most, to the attacks of individual zeal. And yet there is no doubt that here, even more than with political grievances, the combined exertions of many would do far more than the utmost energy of isolated virtue. Nor is such an association merely visionary; on the contrary, there has existed one for eighteen hundred years; it has spread itself over all the countries of Europe; England, amongst the rest, is well acquainted with its name: almost every Englishman within the four seas professes to belong to it. This great society, for the putting down of moral evil, is no other than the Church of Christ.

Now I would wish every reader to ask himself whether this idea of the Church of Christ appears strange to him or natural? If the former, then let him consider whether it ought to seem strange to him;—whether, if he consults the Scriptures, he will not find this notion of Christianity everywhere prominent; whether the most peculiar ordinances of the Christian religion are not grounded upon it and imply it. And let him think again, whether it is not likely, if the true nature of the Church be so different from what he has imagined it to be, that its practical results may possibly be of a kind which he has never as yet anticipated; may he not suspect, in short, that all his views of what is called religion have been injured by this original misapprehension? Or again, if the reader is prepared to admit that Christ's Church is a society for the putting down of moral evil, let him ask himself whether he has well considered the legitimate consequences of such a definition of it; whether, in fact, it is not practically forgotten; and whether that comparative failure of Christianity as to its effects upon the world, which all Christians acknowledge and lament, may not possibly be owing to this constant practical misunderstanding of its true character?

It will be found, I think, that neither in their use of the word "Religion," nor in speaking of "the Church," do men in general form any idea of the social character of Christianity. With "Religion" this is manifest; for, indeed, the term properly expresses nothing more than certain relations of man towards God, without intimating that these are necessarily involved with a peculiar relation of men to each other. "The Church" is spoken of in various senses, and with great vagueness; still it may be safely affirmed that it is not commonly understood to mean "the Society of Christians," but rather a distinct institution for the benefit of that society in one particular way, namely, their religious benefit: so that it is either taken as synonymous with "the Clergy," or with "a provision for the religious instruction of a people by public teaching and ceremonies." Both these meanings, it will be seen, are very different from that of "a Society for the putting down of moral evil," and the points of difference are the exact measure of the inferiority of these false notions of "the Church of Christ" to the true one.

For if "the Church" be "the society of Christians," then every Christian is a member of the Church, a member of a society, whose objects are his objects, its interests are his interests, and in whose concerns he is therefore called upon to take an active part, and not merely a passive one. And, again, if the object of the Church be called "religious instruction," then a great portion of human life is taken away from its regard: its business is made particular, and not general; it is one amongst many of the institutions which society needs, instead of being society itself, in its most exalted relation, engaged in the perfecting of our moral nature. It is, therefore, of some importance, to ascertain whether these great weakenings of the efficacy and limitations of the range of the Church of Christ be according to the purpose for which it was founded.

That the Church of Christ was intended to be a society of which all Christians were to be members, and all active and useful towards the great object of the society, appears, to quote one passage out of a great number, from the twelfth chapter of St. Paul's Epistle to the Corinthians. The Church is there compared to the human body, which consists indeed of various members, but all active: if any were merely passive, and acted upon by other parts of the body, the healthy constitution of the whole would be impaired. The members indeed have different offices, but none may despise the rest, or can do without them. And lest this comparison might, in one respect, lead to error, because, in the human body, according to popular notions, there resides such a sovereignty and superiority in the brain or head, that in respect of its great activity, some of the other members may be called passive; therefore, the functions of the head in the Christian Church are assigned exclusively[a] to Christ

[a] " It is this point—that Christ is the Head of the Church—which will greatly help us to understand what is meant by the Church. For as Christ is not upon earth, nor exercises any visible government, nor is present in one place more than another, and yet is truly the Head and Governor of His Church, so we see at once that His Church is not to be thought of as a society or government in the common meaning of the words; but in that other sense in which we speak of civil society and of God's moral government, to the first of which all men who are not savages belong, while to

himself, and all Christians are said to be members one of another, forming jointly that body, of which as at the other all men whatsoever are subject. And as all civilized men belong to civilized society, and acknowledge in many respects a common law—although, in another sense, they belong to a great many different societies, and have very different laws—so it is with Christian men and with religious society. In that sense in which the Church has Christ for its Head, and is the Temple of the Holy Ghost, all Christians belong to it and all acknowledge one common law; while in another sense Christians belong to a great many different churches, and those churches have a great many different laws.

" But it is in its first and highest sense that the Church of Christ is the Communion of all living Christians -- that it is Christ's mystical body, holy and beloved—the Heir of the promises, the Israel of God, against which the gates of hell shall not prevail. To the end of the world as there will be civilized society on earth, so will there be Christian society. Men will not all be savages, nor all strangers to God; there will be those who shall love one another for Christ's sake, who shall own one Spirit and one Lord and one God; who shall be striving against one and the same spiritual enemy, and walking together in one and the same hope of life eternal."
—*Extract from a MS. Sermon on All Saints' Day*, 1835.

To the same effect are some remarks in a letter to Dr. Hawkins, November, 1830. " Have you ever clearly defined to yourself what you mean by 'one society,' as applied to the whole Christian Church upon earth? It seems to me that most of what I consider the errors about ' the Church,' turn upon an imperfect understanding of this point. In one sense, and that a very important one, all Christians belong to one society; but then it is more like Cicero's sense of ' societas,' than what we mean by a society. There is a ' societas generis humani,' and a ' societas hominum Christianorum;' but there is not one ' respublica' or 'civitas' of either, but a great many. The Roman Catholics say there is but one 'respublica,' and therefore, with perfect consistency, they say that there must be one central government: our Article, if I mistake not its sense, says, and with great truth, that the Christian Respublica depends on the political Respublica; that is, that there may be at least as many Christian societies as there are political societies, and that there may be, and in our own kingdom are, even more. If there be one Christian society, in the common sense of the word, there must be one government; whereas, in point of fact, the Scotch Church, the English Church, and the French Church, have all separate and perfectly independent governments; and consequently can only be in an unusual and peculiar sense ' one society': that is, spiritually one, as having the same objects, and the same principles, and the same supports, and the same enemies."—*Life and Correspondence*, vol. i. pp. 277, 78, 4th edition.

once connected with it, yet essentially superior and sovereign over it, Christ alone is fitted to be the Head.

Christ's Church, then, was to be a society, all whose members were to be active in promoting the society's objects. And this object was to be the putting down of moral evil, both within the Church and without it. It was to be the leaven to leaven the world, clearly that is, to change its moral character; and, with respect to its operations upon itself, how magnificently is it described as working by the grace of its divine Head through the instrumentality of every joint and member performing its own portion of the work, to its own growth in truth and in love, in intellectual and moral perfection, according to no less a standard than the perfection of nature of Christ Himself, the All-wise and the Most Holy. For this, the members each separately, and the body all together, are to labour together with their Lord, that the Church, this great society, may become fully glorious; "not having spot or wrinkle or any such thing, but holy and without blemish."

There is, then, a society in existence, for the putting down of all moral evil, by the combined exertions of all its members. This society is the Church of Christ, and every Christian in England is a member of it. How is it that we have not rightly appreciated our relations and duties as such? How is it that the Church amongst us retains so faint a resemblance to a society, and works with such insufficient efficacy, nay, apparently with so inadequate a conception of its true object? The explanation of the fact is humiliating indeed, but it ought to be most instructive.

CHAPTER II.

Before, however, we proceed to the explanation of the fact, it will be proper to develope and expose more fully to the observation of the reader the actual features of the fact itself. That is, having seen what is the true notion of the Church of Christ, " a society for the putting down of moral evil," or " for the moral improvement of mankind," let us examine how far the existing state of the Church amongst us is agreeable to this definition of it.

First of all, instead of one Church or society of Christians, we find a multitude. I do not mean that there are a number of particular congregations locally distinct, and therefore distinct also in their administration and municipal government. This might be the case without the slightest breach of Christian unity; and all these, in one sense, distinct societies would yet, in the true Christian sense, belong to one and the same. But we find not only distinction and municipal independence, but moral alienation. The different Christian societies amongst us are not distinct for the sake of local convenience, or a more satisfactory administration of their respective concerns; but because they disapprove of each other religiously; because each thinks that the others have injured the perfection of Christianity by some improper addition or omission; that, in short, they could not satisfactorily worship God together: and therefore there is something in their mutual feelings which goes beyond distinctness; there exists, to say the very least, something of alienation; they feel in some degree opposed to one another. The prosperity of any one of them is not a matter of unmixed rejoicing to the rest, nor its decline a matter of unmixed regret.

Now it is manifest that such feelings existing between several societies must so far hinder them from acting in common; so far as men disapprove of one another religiously, they will be backward in acting together in religious matters. So that here we have the Church of Christ truly divided, because it is divided morally; because men are less inclined to work together for the objects of that Church. And as division in the sense of disagreement is weakness, even to a proverb, so the Church of Christ is weakened in its actual existence amongst us, because it has ceased morally to be one society.

Again, take the several societies of Christians amongst us, and consider how far their avowed object seems to be the putting down of moral evil. Are they not rather societies formed for what is called religious edification? i. e. for instructing their members in religious truth? or for the joint indulgence and expression of their devotional feelings? or for supplying their members with the comforts and consolations of religion as purely as possible? Doubtless these are amongst the objects for which the Church was formed; or, to speak more properly, these are the necessary means for the accomplishing of its object. Religious instruction, the exercises of prayer and praise, the participation in the sacraments, are amongst the prescribed and most necessary means for our growth in goodness. Still it is most essential that they should always be clearly seen to be means, and not in themselves an end; that their bearing is upon human life and character; that they belong to the Church of Christ as its instruments, and that the Church was founded, not merely for the perfecting these instruments, but for their application after being perfected; that its members should worship together, in order to live together; and that their combined efforts are wanted, not only for sowing the seed, but for cherishing the plant and reaping the harvest; that the Church, in short, is more for the week-days than for the Sunday; more for the house, the street, or the field, than for that particular building which, by an unfortunate ambiguity of language, has appropriated to itself its name.

Further, not only is the object of the Christian Church unduly narrowed, but its character has been almost forgotten. When we speak of the actual Church, at least of the Established Church, as a society, we give it a title which the reality will scarcely warrant. The social character has been lost sight of, because the ministry has been corrupted into a priesthood, and has thus almost monopolized the active functions of the whole body. The term "society" is inapplicable to a despotism, or to an anarchy; it matters not whether those in authority have a tyrannical power, or an inefficient one, if they alone are active, and no regular means are provided by which the other members of the body may support them, encourage them, direct them, or control them; if, in short, the whole business of the body, be it much or little, is delegated to them exclusively, then the excellences and uses of a society are forfeited; we lose not only its freedom, but its energy; we have no longer the combined action of many, contributing their varied powers and their joint interest to the promotion of the common good,—but the isolated power of a few, acting sometimes violently, but always imperfectly, upon a mass in itself inert and neutral.

The existing Church, then, falls short of the definition of the pure Christian Church, that it is " a society for the putting down of moral evil," from two causes: first, because it has substituted for its true object another, less extensive, and much more liable to be perverted; and secondly, because it has in a great measure abandoned its social character, and become an order rather than a society. In other words, it has unduly limited, and otherwise unduly corrupted its notions of Christian doctrine, and has well nigh destroyed the efficacy of its Church government; and therefore, as a means of acting upon mankind in the mass, it has greatly failed; failed not absolutely, but in comparison with what it might have effected had it properly availed itself of its divine powers. It has not put down evil, for evil in the course of this world is still predominant; it has but softened some of its worst features, so far as regards mankind as a whole; while the fulness of its blessings has been tasted only by individuals: that is to say, that the good done has been wrought by Christianity; the good not done has been lost by the imperfections of the Christian Church.

CHAPTER III.

In saying that " the Church has unduly limited and unduly extended its notions of Christian doctrine," the general misunderstanding to which this statement would be liable, is in itself, the best confirmation of its truth. We commonly mean by " doctrine," something different from the proper Christian meaning of the word, and therefore, the charge of unduly limiting or extending it, would be also interpreted erroneously, and when so misinterpreted, would be easily refuted. " An undue limitation, and an undue extension of Christian doctrine," would be commonly understood to mean, " that certain doctrines necessary to salvation were not taught, and that others not necessary to salvation were taught as necessary;" but then by the term " doctrines" would be understood, "truths revealed in Scripture relating to the nature of God or to his dealings with mankind," as distinct from "truths relating to man's principles and duties." Now, from this erroneous idea of Christian doctrine, there have flowed the very evils of which I have spoken: it has been limited and extended unduly, because its nature has been mistaken, because its predominant character has been supposed to be "truth," whereas it is in fact, " efficacy as a means of moral good."

The object of Christianity is to save men's souls; and as this can only be done by changing them from evil to good; by altering their hopes, and fears, and affections; so, the immediate object of Christianity is, to produce in men a moral and spiritual improvement, in scriptural language, to create them after a new and better nature. Now, when this improvement is sought to be effected by direct precepts, Christian doctrine is no more than a law of duties, a statement of what we ought to do, and what we ought not to do. When it is to be effected by an appeal to our hopes and fears, Christian doctrine must be a statement of certain facts, tending to excite hope and fear; a declaration of some good to be gained, of some evil to be avoided. Further, when the improvement is to be effected by strengthening our moral powers, or by purifying and increasing our affections, Christian doctrine must teach us the way by which this moral strength may be gained, and present to our minds certain facts and objects fitted to be the perfect food of our best affections, to nourish them, to give them intensity, and to mingle in them no element of evil. Thus, while Christian doctrine will not be one in substance nor in kind, it will be one in object: its instruments will, in themselves, be varied, but, as regards the use which it makes of them, they will be similar; they belong to Christian doctrine only, so far as they all alike minister to the moral and spiritual improvement of man.

This scriptural view of Christian doctrine exhibits it as no less admirable in its proportions than in the matter which it inculcates. The mixture of direct precept with the revelation of facts or characters calculated to produce a certain moral effect, seems to meet exactly all the wants of our nature; enlightening us, strengthening us, and enkindling us, all at once. But, instead of this view, another has been too generally adopted. First, all the direct precepts have been struck off from Christian doctrine, and put under another head, that of practical instruction; implying, that Christian doctrine had some other end than that of practical improvement. Secondly, doctrine thus reduced to the revelation of certain facts, was further corrupted by being made to declare these facts as simple truths, apart from the impression which they were meant to produce on men; and being thus brought to deliver theorems, instead of motives and principles of life, was again corrupted still more by being loaded with new truths, supposed to be deduced by a fair process of reasoning from certain expressions in the Scripture, but which being incapable of a moral bearing upon the heart and character, were no part of the real Christian doctrine, and therefore cannot be proved from Scripture with such clearness, as to prevent great doubts and exceptions from being made against them. And so it is, that Christian doctrine has been unduly limited and unduly extended; unduly limited, in having all the direct commands of the Scripture struck off from it, and classed under another head: and unduly extended, in being made to contain certain truths, which, as having no practical tendency, were never designed by Christ to constitute any part of it.

Now that Christian doctrine does properly include the direct practical precepts of our Lord and His Apostles may be shown without difficulty. As far as any stress may be laid on the use of a word, "doctrine," διδαχή, in the great majority of passages in which it occurs in the New Testament, signifies practical teaching, such as that of our Lord's parables, or His sermon on the Mount. And without referring to the word, it is clear that the substance of our Lord's teaching during His ministry, as well as that of His Apostles' teaching after His ascension, was of a practical character. Again in that invaluable picture of the proceedings of the early Christians, which is given in Pliny's famous letter to Trajan, it appears that a principal object of their assemblies amongst themselves was, to pledge themselves to one another to abstain from everything evil, and to live soberly, honestly, and godly. It must needs have formed no small part of their doctrine to explain and impress upon the new converts the nature and importance of the things which they thus pledged themselves to abstain from, or to do.

Again, there is an important benefit obtained by making the precepts of the Gospel a main part of Christian doctrine, that it shows how large a portion of this doctrine is received by all Christians with perfect unanimity. The differences of opinion as to the meaning and force of the moral precepts of Scripture are so trifling as hardly to deserve notice; and thus George Herbert says truly:

> " All the doctrine, which Christ taught and gave,
> Was clear as Heav'n from whence it came;
> At least those beams of truth, which only save,
> Surpass in brightness any flame.

"' Love God and love your neighbour. Watch and pray.
Do as you would be done unto.'
Oh ! dark instructions, even as dark as day !
Who can these Gordian knots undo?"

But George Herbert should have remembered that these " bright and saving beams of truth," as he well calls them, were excluded from the common meaning of the term " Christian doctrine" in its technical and corrupt sense; and that that doctrine was made to consist of many points far less bright and less saving; points which alone could offer any ground for the unbeliever's taunt, that Christians could not agree as to the tenets of their own religion.

[Here the MS. breaks off.—But the subject of the concluding chapter of it may receive some further illustration from the following portion of a pamphlet, which, in 1835, he wrote but never published, " On the Admission of Dissenters to the Universities," in the form of a letter to the Rev. W. K. Hamilton, and which, though written with reference to the particular question of academical instruction, is evidently a developement of the same thoughts which have been expressed in the foregoing fragment[a].]

Now it is this habit of completing Scripture, of altering the order and the proportions of its doctrines, which has led to the apparent differences in men's interpretations of it. There has constantly been a tacit reference to some other standard, to which some have laboured to make the Scripture conform, while others have striven to make it as different from it as possible. Thus men have come to regard it as impossible to interpret the Scriptures to persons of different religious opinions ; and so it is impossible, as long as a foreign standard of interpretation is constantly before the eyes

[a] See also Letters to Rev. J. Hearn and Rev. A. Hare, May and August, 1833. (*Life and Correspondence*, 4th edition, vol. i. pp. 361, 368.) and Sermon on " Christian Prophesying." (*Sermons*, vol. vi. p. 289.

of all, and exciting in them the most opposite feelings. If you were to lecture on the first chapter of St. John to a class partly consisting of Unitarians, and were to dwell on it as proving the truth of the Nicene Creed, the party feelings of the Unitarians would be directly excited; they would take refuge in Lardner's interpretation of the passage, and would be perfectly insensible to its real and simple meaning. But dropping all thoughts of Trinitarianism and Unitarianism,—looking upon all around you as Christians, engaged with you in receiving the instruction of Christ's beloved disciple,— and considering no further deductions from the Apostle's words than he himself intended to follow from them, would not the words in their own simple force convey all that you wish, and if you forbore from making them controversial, would they not make their own way into a Unitarian's mind, and show him that he does not at present regard his Master with the same reverence that St. John regarded Him?

Suppose this to be carried on further; that the greatest part of the New Testament were thus simply interpreted, with no other end in view than that of impressing to the utmost on your pupils the particular view or feeling which each portion successively was designed to convey: at the same time that in all your lectures sound rules and habits of criticism are communicated, while Christian hopes and principles are continually brought forward, as naturally suggested by the study of the human mind under different influences and guidance: would your Unitarian pupils at the end of their three years be as much Unitarian as they were at the beginning? Would they not at any rate be perfectly ashamed of the ignorance and unfairness of their own pretended "improved" version of the New Testament,— would they not feel that Christ was not in their system what

He was in the minds of the Apostles, that if the language of St. Paul and St. John be not the wildest exaggeration, that of their own sect must be cold even to irreverence? I do not say that they would subscribe to the Articles of the Church of England—that they might feel to be going over to an opposite party—but their religion would be far more Scriptural and entirely Christian than it had been at their first coming to the University, and their influence in life, be it more or less, would soften and improve the character of their sect, or, at least, would act beneficially on their own children. They would have reason to look back upon Oxford with gratitude, and their teachers might thank God to the latest hour of their lives that they had been enabled to communicate truth and charity to minds, which, irritated by a system of exclusion, and trained up in sectarian narrowness, would have drunk deeper and deeper of error and of bitterness.

Or again, for the members of our own Church;—would they be injured by a similar system of instruction,—would they be worse Christians, or worse members of the Church of England than they are likely to become under the influence of that spirit which is now but too prevalent among you? Worse Christians they could not be, if the Scriptures are indeed our standard of Christianity; nor would they be worse churchmen, unless a narrow spirit of religious and political party, perpetuating divisions, and thus hindering the Church from becoming national and effective, be a true zeal for the welfare of Christ's Church established in this kingdom. Their admiration of the Liturgy and Articles of our present constitution would be—I had almost said less idolatrous,—than it seems to be now; but it would be more sincere and abundantly better grounded. True it is, that knowing that both

c

additions and omissions were made in the original Articles of the Church of England within ten years of their first publication, they would probably judge that the lapse of two hundred and seventy years must have made other additions and omissions expedient now; remembering that the Liturgy was altered several times in a Christian spirit, that the last nominal revision in 1661-2 was the mere mockery of a triumphant party, and that the revision attempted in 1689 by some of the best men in our church was frustrated by the influence of the same party, they would probably desire another revision in the spirit of 1689 to be carried into effect now. But they would preserve the substance both of the Liturgy and Articles as earnestly as they would revise and endeavour to improve them: they would feel deeply and thankfully the positive truth contained in the one, and the piety and wisdom and eloquence of the other; they would admire that rejection of errors on the right hand and on the left, in which the English Reformers so eminently displayed their fairness and their judgment.

Taking, however, a simpler view of the case, I believe that the religious instruction of every individual under-graduate would be far purer and more effectual than it now is, if the thirty-nine Articles were never presented to them as a subject of study, but the Scriptures were made the only text-book in what are called Divinity Lectures, whilst the Catechism furnished the outline for any more private and personal instruction that was given to individuals. There can be no more fatal error, none certainly more entirely at variance with the Scripture model, than to acquaint the mind with the truths of religion in a theoretical form, leaving the application of them to be made afterwards. On the contrary, the practical form is not only that in which they should be first communicated, but in many instances they should never be put into the abstract form at all, and if they are so put, they become misleading. An à priori religion is a very different thing from Christianity; the Gospel is founded on man's wants and weaknesses, and the revelations of God are exactly commensurate with these wants, and go no farther. Look at the first of our Articles, and compare it with the Scriptural way of putting before us the very same truths. Every thing in the Article is abstract, it contains a series of propositions precisely of that sort which the devils may believe and yet still be devils; the assent given to them need not have any thing of the character of Christian faith. Now if we turn to those passages of Scripture which would be referred to as authorities for the truth of the Article, the difference in the manner of putting the several propositions is remarkable. The unity of God which is so often insisted on, is taught as a corrective of Polytheism; we are not to worship a variety of superior beings with a divided worship; it is not that there is one God in Israel and another in Syria, that one Being made the world and another governs it; but all our religious feelings of hope and fear, of love and of honour, should be directed to One alone, the Lord of life and death alike,— the God of our first fathers no less than our own. Thus with regard to Christians, the unity of God should be taught as condemning all superstitious worship of saints or angels, and as a call to missionary labours: for God being the God of all the earth, all should be taught to know Him; but when put as a metaphysical fact with regard to the Divine nature, we have seen it actually lead to error, as in the case of the Unitarians. Again, "God is without body, parts, or passions." Most true certainly; yet even this is put differently in the Scripture,—not as a truth, but as a lesson: "God is a Spirit, and they that worship Him must worship Him in spirit and in truth." Yet more with the conclusion of the Article: does the Scripture ever speak of the Trinity as of a fact, so to speak, in the Divine existence? Does not its language always refer to the various relations of God with ourselves? In this respect the language of the Catechism is exactly Scriptural. "I learn to believe in God the Father who hath made me, in God the Son who hath redeemed me, in God the Holy Ghost who hath sanctified me;" that is to say, our notions of God should never for an instant be separated from our own personal relations to Him. And if the external evidence were less decisive against it, the internal would of itself be sufficient in my judgment to throw strong suspicion on the famous verse of the Three Heavenly Witnesses; the abstract declaration of the relations of the Father, Son, and Holy Spirit to one another, (for their unity does not bear[a] upon their witness, but is mentioned as a thing by itself,) appearing to me to be at variance with the character of the revelations of Scripture.

I am led to think that this distinction, between the putting of the doctrines of Christianity in the shape of abstract truths and conveying them as lessons, is one of no small importance, because I observe that the Scripture constantly adopts the latter mode, while the great

[a] For when, on another occasion, the Father and the Son are spoken of as witnesses, they are purposely represented as *two* and not as *one*, in accommodation to our notion that the number of witnesses increases the credibility of the thing attested. "It is written in your law that the testimony of two men is true. I am one that bear witness of myself, and the Father that sent me beareth witness of me." But when the point aimed at is to produce entire trust in Christ's power, then His unity with the Father is declared, not as an abstract truth, but as a practical one. "I and my Father are one." [1 John v. 7. John viii. 17, 18; x. 30.]

disputes amongst Christians have manifestly arisen out of the prevalence of the former. For one of the most fruitful sources of dispute has been the habit of making deductions from Scripture; a practice which is reasonable or unreasonable, according to the nature and object of the Gospel revelations. If they are meant to declare the absolute existence of certain truths, then we may properly make deductions from these truths, exactly as we do in human philosophy. But if the truths declared are wholly relative and practical, then we may not make abstract deductions from them, because abstractedly nothing has been revealed about them, and we may only use them for the purpose for which they are used in Scripture, that is, as producing a certain particular moral impression on our minds,—not as declaring some positive truth in the nature of things. This is understood clearly with regard to parables, where we see at once that they convey a lesson and not a fact, and that beyond the special lesson intended to be communicated we can draw no deductions from them. But I think, that in proportion to our increased knowledge and study of the Scriptures, will be our conviction that something of this sort applies, and must apply, to all revelations concerning God and heavenly things; and that it is by so reading the Scripture that we derive the entire impression of the mind of the Spirit: not finding embarrassment, but rather great instruction and benefit in those passages, which, taken as declaring abstract truths, appear so opposite as to be almost irreconcileable, and which, therefore, have given support to the most opposite theories, when in reality none of them warrant our forming any general theory at all.[a]

Again the study of articles of religion is injurious in

[a] [See Sermons, vol. iii. p. 395; vol. iv. pp. 290, 377.]

this respect, that it confirms that narrow and unscriptural use of the term "doctrine" which has been too long adopted in common language. To speak of the doctrines of the Gospel, as opposed to its precepts, is unscriptural and mischievous. If you take the trouble to observe the signification of the words, διδαχὴ, διδασκαλία, διδάσκω, &c., in the various passages of the New Testament in which they are to be found, you will see that in the very great majority of instances they are applied particularly to what we call the precepts of the Gospel; in others they embrace the whole mass of Christian instruction,—*i. e.*, Christian practice and feelings enforced on Christian principles; but that most rarely, (I believe I might say "never," were I not always unwilling to assert a negative universally,) most rarely do they signify what we technically call doctrines,—*i. e.*, general truths of religion. The Articles may contain a full view of Christian doctrine in this technical sense of the word, but in the Scriptural sense they contain a most meagre and imperfect view of it. Indeed it is to be observed that the only notice which they take of the great moral peculiarities of Christian doctrine, is to notice certain exceptions to Christ's general rules; so that in studying the Articles we do not find the Christian doctrine enforced, but only a protest entered against certain exaggerated views of it. But is it no mischief that a young man's attention should be only directed to the Christian doctrine concerning oaths, in order to teach him that some oaths may lawfully be taken; whereas no man can doubt that the exception had far better be neglected than the rule; and f the Christian doctrine against the principle of oaths in general, and therefore against the imposition of them by Christian governments, had been enforced as it should have been, Christian reform in these matters, which the Bishop of London is now so nobly advocating, would not have been delayed till the nineteenth century? The same may be said with respect to the Christian doctrine relating to war and capital punishments. The exceptions made in the Articles are true as exceptions, but by dwelling on them we have lost the benefit of the rule; and it surely better becomes the Christian Church to enforce with all its power the principle of its Lord's doctrine,—a doctrine so unwelcome to our natural evil, and so greatly needed,—rather than to content itself with a caution against pushing this doctrine into extravagance. If the Scripture itself be our text-book, we find all this given in its proper proportions; but on the present system it is perfectly possible for a man to study carefully what we call Christian doctrines, and yet to have a most inadequate notion of Christian doctrine in the Scriptural sense of the term,—the doctrine of Christian feelings and Christian principles and practice." . . . .

(B.) THE STATE AND THE CHURCH.

Written in 1833, 34. See Letters to Archbishop Whately and Mr. Hull, in April and July, 1834. (Life and Correspondence, vol. i. pp. 385, 391. 4th edit.)

CHAPTER I.

THE relations of what are called the State and the Church to each other, have been more or less matter of dispute in every period of modern history. At this moment nothing is so vague as the opinions generally entertained respecting them: and such as are not vague appear to me to be only definitely erroneous. It may be very true abstractedly that the importance of the subject requires to be discussed at length; but a long work upon it would find but few readers. Now the erroneous views entertained upon it are conveyed, not in long and detailed arguments, but in short addresses, which may be read through in half an hour. When error dogmatizes, truth may be allowed to do the same. If ever the propagators of error will venture to expound at length the grounds of their system, it will then be time enough for the grounds on which the truth rests to be stated at length in answer.

The great errors which I here purpose to combat are two: one relating to the State, and the other to the Church.

The first, as entertained by a far more numerous and powerful body than the other, is by much the most dangerous; in fact, the great danger of the other error consists in its tendency to lead practically to the establishment of this. Now this first error consists in lowering and limiting the duty and business of the State; it teaches "that the State, as such, is of no religion;" "that its business is simply to look after the bodies of men; to provide for the security of their persons and property; and that, therefore, it may and ought to leave the concerns of religion to individuals, and to make no public provision for its maintenance." I do not mean to say that all who have held the premises here mentioned have also held the conclusion; on the contrary, Warburton held them, and contended strongly at the same time for the expediency of having an established religion; nor have there been wanting others who have taken a similar course. But the general tendency has been and is to hold the premises and conclusion together, nay, to value the premises chiefly for the very reason because they seem to authorize such a conclusion.

Now in determining what are the objects and business of a State in the abstract, history gives us little direct assistance. The actual origin of civilized society in every country, so far as we can trace it, belongs to circumstances much more than to design. And descending to later times, the objects of different governments have been so various, and pursued so inconsistently by the same government at different periods, that we know not where to look for our standard. But there is one attribute which seems essential to a State, —namely, sovereignty. A State has no earthly superior; the law, which is the State's voice, is supreme over all the members of the State, and its sentence can take from them both their property and their lives. A power so extensive must necessarily reach to every part of human life; all our actions in every period of our existence must be done either by its command or with its permission.

When, therefore, Warburton speaks of civil policy requiring the aid of religion and entering into alliance with it because of its own necessary imperfections, such for instance, as its inability to reward virtue, or to punish every kind of moral evil, he might just as reasonably talk of its entering into alliance with medicine, or with agriculture, or with political economy, because human society requires the benefits of these and of all other arts and sciences. If we must speak in metaphors, the State does not ally itself with them, but employs their services: fixes their respective places, and when their counsels are at variance with each other, determines of its sovereign pleasure which it shall follow. The essence of a State is power; what is no more than advice when spoken by philosophy and religion, binding, so far as this world is concerned, only on those who choose to follow it,—that, when adopted by the State, becomes law, and so far as this world is concerned, no man can disobey it with impunity.

An authority, then, so essentially sovereign over human life, controlling every thing, and itself subject to no earthly control, must naturally have a proportionate responsibility. Standing as it were in the place of God, it should imitate God's government wherever the imperfections of humanity do not render such imitation impossible. It seems then an uncalled for assertion, to maintain that it should regard the bodies of men only,—that it should limit the exercise of its power to the prevention of attacks upon persons and property,—that its highest functions should be those of a minister of police. The doctrine of the old philosophers is surely better in accordance with its sovereignty. They taught that as its power extended over the whole of human life, so human happiness, in the largest sense of the word, was its proper object; not physical happiness only, and much less the prevention of outward violence, but that compound happiness which belongs to man as a compound being,—the happiness conferred by wisdom and virtue, no less than the comfort which is derived from food and clothing.

Warburton speaks as if civil society had been formally instituted with the avowed object of procuring some one definite end; which end, he tells us, was " security to the temporal liberty and property of man."[a] Now to speak of any such formal institution of society as a matter of fact, is as far from the truth as to speak of " an original compact between the magistrate and the people," as if such a compact had literally been signed and sealed between them. The actual beginnings of society neither conceived of its object that it was merely " security to temporal liberty and property," nor that it was " the highest happiness attainable by man." If political society ever grew directly out of patriarchal, the predominant notion attached to the

[a] [Warburton's Alliance of Church and State, book i. chap. 4.]

office of king would be that undefined one of general dignity and dominion which nature attaches to the character of a father. If, as is more probable, it grew out of conquest, the notion again was likely to be that of dominion, without any distinct conception of the ends for which that dominion was to be exercised; the conquerors desired power, and the conquered to escape worse evils submitted to it. Afterwards, when sovereignty had thus arisen, its capabilities, whether for good or for evil, were gradually developed: good men found that it enabled them to promote the happiness of mankind by improving their condition physically and morally; bad men found it convenient for the purposes of their own rapacity or ambition, and converted it into a tyranny. But because some degree of security for liberty and property is the minimum of good which sovereignty can confer without being guilty of self-destruction,—for tyranny undoes itself if it opens to every one its monopoly of oppression,—therefore governments which have cared for no higher object have yet necessarily repressed indiscriminate violence amongst their people; and the lowest good attainable by society has, as was natural, been more frequently pursued by States actually than the higher good which it may and ought to attain, but which implies that its rulers should be, what too often they have not been, men sensible of the excellence of wisdom and virtue.

Warburton allows, indeed, that the State is concerned with morals, so far as they affect men's outward interests; nay, even with [a] "the three fundamental principles of natural religion, namely, the being of a God, His providence over human affairs, and the natural essential difference between moral good and evil." "These doctrines," he goes on to say, "it is directly of the magistrate's office to cherish, protect, and *propagate;*

---

[a] [Warburton's Alliance of Church and State, book i. chap. 4.]

". . . . Nor doth this at all contradict our general position, that the sole end of civil society is *the conservation of body and goods*. For the magistrate concerns himself with the maintenance of these three fundamental articles, not as they promote *our future happiness*, but *our present*, as they are the very foundation and bond of civil policy." So then the State may and ought to employ the services of philosophy and religion; but it must do so only to prostitute them both: it must uphold the essential difference of moral good and evil, so far only as it is morally evil to assault our neighbour's person or to rob him of his property, and morally good to abstain from doing so: it must teach that God is, and that He is a rewarder of them who diligently seek Him, only to show its people that they cannot with impunity swear a false oath on a trial or at the custom-house!

There are three points which seem particularly to have misled Warburton's mind into such conclusions as these. First, the confusion of the term "temporal" or "present happiness," with "security to temporal liberty and property;" secondly, "the inability of the State to reward virtue;" and, thirdly, "its punishing evil or other principles than those of pure morality and religion."

I. The confusion in his use of the term "temporal or present happiness," is apparent in the passage which I have quoted above. "Present happiness" is surely not synonymous with "the conservation of body and goods," nor is it necessarily opposed to "future happiness." The immediate object of every earthly society must be "present good," because "future good" can thus only be obtained. But man's highest[a] present good is the same in kind with his future good,—being the perfection of his intellectual and moral nature. This, however, is very far from synonymous with the "conserva-

[a] [See Lectures on Mod. Hist. 3rd edit. p. 55.]

tion of his body and goods," and although we may readily grant that the immediate object of a State is man's present happiness, yet it would by no means follow from this that it was limited to the security of his body and goods from external violence.

II. The State cannot reward virtue, it must "borrow the sanction of rewards from religion." Now it is undoubtedly impossible for society to apportion happiness and misery to its members exactly according to their moral deservings. There are many things good and evil of which God keeps the distribution wholly to himself. I said above, therefore, that "the State should imitate God's government so far as the imperfections of humanity permitted." But it may be doubted whether Warburton is correct in understanding by "reward," "such as is conferred on every one for observing the laws of his country;" as distinguished from "such as is bestowed on particulars for any eminent service." For "laws," in the common sense of the term, prohibiting evil rather than enjoining good, the observance of them is no more than the bare abstaining from evil; and abstaining from evil has its fit return, not in "reward," but in "not being subject to punishment." Now if exemption from punishment be reward, then the State can and does reward those who observe its laws: but if reward mean, as it does naturally, "the bestowing of some positive good," then it is no imputation upon the State that it does not confer such positive good on the negative merit of not doing evil.

But if we choose to take the term "laws"[a] in the wider sense of the old philosophers, and understand by it, not such as are written only, but also the unwritten, —not such as merely forbid evil, but such as enjoin all

[a] [See Inaugural Lecture in the " Lectures on Mod. Hist." p. 14. 3rd edit.]

good, then the State is capable of rewarding in some degree the observance of its laws; negatively, by repressing those wrongs and violences which obstruct the natural tendency of virtue to confer happiness; and, positively, by creating such a state of public opinion as shall ensure to every man in proportion to his goodness an adequate share of a great external comfort,—namely, the esteem, and regard, and reverence of his fellows.

Again, supposing that the State could in no sense reward virtue, it avails Warburton's argument nothing to say, that it must "borrow the sanction of rewards from religion." For in order to serve his purpose, "religion" must be synonymous with "religious society," *i.e.*, with the Church. But the Church is as destitute of the sanction of rewards as the State, since it has lost the miraculous gift of healing. All that it can give is that which does not belong to it in virtue of its being a society; not the sanction of rewards as conferred by itself now, but the belief in such a sanction as to be manifested by God hereafter to all who have loved Him and worked righteousness. This "borrowing from religion" is of the same sort with the "borrowings from philosophy," "political economy," &c., which the State may have occasion for, without our confounding the nature of its sovereignty, or supposing that it must or can contract an alliance with a society of philosophers or economists.

III. "The State punishes evil on other principles than those of morality and religion." This, I think, is the main difficulty which has induced many persons to agree with Warburton in his low estimate of the objects of civil society. But the point to be considered is whether this imputation is one which peculiarly touches the State, or whether it does not arise from those imperfections of humanity which are incident to every society composed of human beings. For instance, when it is said that the State does not punish some kinds of sensual indulgences, it is merely saying that public opinion has never yet been sufficiently pure in such matters as to allow of their punishment. It is a fault incident alike to civil and to religious society when existing on a large scale, in other words when they do not consist merely of a small number of picked individuals. The reason which Warburton alleges, that by checking severely one class of offences of this description others of a worse character may be encouraged, applies exactly as much to the Church as to the State, if it be valid in either case. But the purity of morals actually obtained in one sex under present circumstances by the decided demand of public opinion, and the legal punishments actually inflicted on some particular sensualities, sufficiently show that there is no peculiar incapacity in civil society to enforce purity of morals,—but that men, and even Christians, have never yet generally estimated *all* offences against this purity after the measure prescribed alike by reason and revelation.

Again, generally, the State, it is said, punishes evil actions only in proportion to their malignant influence on civil society. The truth is, that the rule followed in practice has mostly been very capricious, as if governments had not been able to satisfy themselves respecting it. They have looked partly at the moral enormity of a crime, partly at its mischievous tendency; and thus the penal legislation of most countries exhibits an inconsistency in its several enactments. Again, it should be recollected that civil society has its indirect inflictions for the breach of its unwritten laws, no less real than the direct penalties by which it secures obedience to its written laws. There are some offences for which loss of character and a tacit exclusion from society are the fittest punishment; and the public opinion which inflicts this is one of society's proper instruments, inasmuch as it is capable of being formed by the institutions and habits which society either enacts or adopts in its practice[a].

But the true reason of such differences as have really existed between human laws and the language of philosophy and religion, is to be found in the fact, that philosophy and religion have exercised so feeble an influence over the bulk of mankind, and that actual governments have, therefore, as I said before, neglected very frequently the higher good which they might have effected, and have confined themselves to that lower sort which was much more generally appreciated. But in so far as they have sometimes, though irregularly and inconsistently, endeavoured after that higher good, they have left as it were on record their acknowledgment of that principle from which their practice, after the usual course of human infirmity, was too often deviating.

Supposing, however, that the influential majority in any State were good and wise men, desirous of promoting the moral and intellectual no less than the physical well-being of their community, their political wisdom, which is the sovereign of all sciences, would undoubtedly avail itself of religion and philosophy to promote the first of these ends, as it would employ political economy, military and naval knowledge, and the various branches of physical science to promote the last. For the sovereign science of human life is that science which is the proper accompaniment of sovereign power;

---

[a] [This argument is more fully developed in "Lect. on Mod. Hist." p. 55. 3rd edit.]

and its business is so to employ the services of all other sciences, that, without interfering with one another, or trying one to exclude the other, they may by their combined efforts, mingled together in just proportions, raise the perfect fabric of human happiness. And therefore the State's sovereign power combined, in the case I am supposing, with the peculiar wisdom which belongs to it, chooses for itself the true religion, as it would choose also the truest system of political science in the lower sense of the term; and in adopting this religion, it declares its belief in its promises and its adherence to its precepts,—in other words it declares itself Christian. But by so doing, it becomes a part of Christ's Holy Catholic Church: not allied with it, which implies distinctness from it, but transformed into it. But as for the particular portion of this Church which may have existed before within the limits of the State's sovereignty,—the actual society of Christian men there subsisting,—the State does not ally itself with such a society,—for alliance supposes two parties equally sovereign,—nor yet does it become the Church as to its outward form and organization; neither does the Church on the other hand become so lost in the State as to become, in the offensive sense of the term, secularized. The spirit of the Church is transfused into a more perfect body, and its former external organization dies away. The form is that of the State, the spirit is that of the Church; what was a kingdom of the world is become a kingdom of Christ, a portion of the Church in the high and spiritual sense of the term; but in that sense in which "Church" denotes the outward and social organization of Christians in any one particular place, it is no longer a Christian Church, but what is far higher and better, a Christian Kingdom. It remains as before,—a sovereign society seeking after

D

its highest happiness; but it has now discovered the true path, and its conceptions as to the nature of its happiness are corrected and exalted. It is changed into a better and a purer self, like [a] Kailyal when she had tasted the Amreeta cup of immortality.

To the view here taken, several objections are or may be made:

First, That it interferes with the political rights of men, by making them to depend on their religious opinions; for if the State, as such, be essentially Christian, those who are not Christians cannot be members of it.

Second, That men being sure to differ in their religious opinions, the State must either become Christian in so vague and general a sense as hardly to deserve the name; or if it adopts the creed of any one particular sect, or frames one distinct and definite for itself, the existence of dissenters will soon embarrass the question, and it will be necessary either to exclude dissenters from their political rights, or to admit the solecism of their legislating for the concerns of the

---

[a] [" She said and drank. The eye of mercy beam'd
Upon the maid: a cloud of fragrance stream'd
Like incense smoke, as all her mortal frame
Dissolved beneath the potent agency
Of that mysterious draught; such quality
From her pure touch the fated cup partook.
   Like one entranced she knelt,
Feeling her body melt
Till all but what was heavenly past away:
   Yet still she felt
Her spirit strong within her—the same heart,
With the same loves, and all her heavenly part
Unchanged and ripened to such perfect state,
In this miraculous birth, as here on earth
Dimly our holiest hopes anticipate."
          (*Southey's Curse of Kehama*, Book xxiv.)]

established religion while they do not hold communion with it.

Third, The Church being essentially distinct from the State ought not to be confounded with it; it may be allied with it, or employed by it, but can never be identified with it.

I. The first objection stirs one of the greatest questions in politics: namely, what is the true bond of political society? or, in other words, what are the qualifications required in a citizen? It also involves another great question—what are the political rights of individuals? To both these questions there is a growing tendency to give an answer, which, as being anarchical and leading to the moral degradation of the human race, may be fitly called Jacobinical.

I need not say how various the qualifications for citizenship have been in different ages and different countries. But was it ever held in the ancient world that a man gained a title to become a citizen by living in a country, acquiring a fortune in it, and paying taxes for the public service? His paying taxes was thought to be no more than a just return for the protection afforded him in a country on which he had no natural claim; nor would any length of time alter the condition of his posterity, unless by a special act of favour on the part of the government. Their services to the State, in bearing a share of the public burdens, could no more remove the natural diversity of their condition than a beast's usefulness to his master could give him a right to be regarded as a man.

Citizenship, in the common course of things, was a matter of race; he was a citizen who was lineally descended from a citizen, and had not forfeited his right by some crime. This was not a mere narrow-minded spirit of family pride. Particular races of men have their own peculiar physical and moral character. They preserved also, in the ancient world, their particular customs, particular moral principles on various important points, and also their particular religion. The mixture of races was accounted a monstrous confusion, introducing a discordance in the habits and principles of a people subversive of political union.

Individuals who obtained the rights of citizenship conformed immediately to the laws, civil and religious, of the country which had adopted them. Individuals might be thus admitted without danger; but the admission of masses of new citizens was considered highly mischievous, as it was likely to shake the existing institutions of the country[a].

This showed a general feeling that the ends of civil society were something higher than mere security to life and property, or facilitating the multiplication of capital. Citizenship implied much more than local neighbourhood, or an intercourse of buying and selling; it was an agreement in the highest feelings and principles of our nature; and certainly Christianity forms so broad a line morally between those who embrace it and other men, that a man who is not a Christian is most justly excluded from citizenship in a Christian state, not merely on grounds furnished by Revelation, but according to the highest and noblest views of the nature of political society.

Again, we hear a great deal too much in the present day of the political rights of *individuals*[b]; this tendency, which is not essentially anarchical, is one of the most distinguishing features of modern civiliza-

---

[a] [See Preface to the third volume of the edition of Thucydides, pp. 15-18. Hist. of Rome, vol. ii. pp. 48-56.]

[b] [See Hist. of Rome, vol. i. p. 265, vol. iii. p. 426.]

tion as distinguished from that of the ancient world [a]. That age of chivalry, whose departure Burke so much regretted, was in one respect the natural parent of that age of Jacobinism which he so much abhorred. Both breathe the spirit of lawlessness, encouraging men to look upon themselves as independent of their fellows; cultivating a proud and selfish idolatry of what belongs to them individually, whether it be personal honour, and personal glory, as in the earlier form of the disease, or personal political liberty and equality as in the later. Both lead to what Bacon calls *bonum suitatis*, to the neglect of the good of the whole body of which we are members. Individuals, in a political sense, are necessarily members; as distinct from the body, they are nothing. Against society, they have no political rights whatever, and their belonging to society or not is a matter not of their own choice, but determined for them by their being born and bred members of it.

II. I approach the second objection with reluctance and shame; for is it not most humiliating that any circumstances should ever have given the slightest colour to the assertion that the term Christian must be vague and of little value, unless some sectarian peculiarities be added to complete the definition?—that to be of Christ is nothing, unless we further declare whether we are of Paul, or Apollos, or Cephas? But so it is; ignorant or dishonest zeal has ever slighted the substance, and idolized the shadow; it is called heresy or indifference to care little for this or that sect's interpretation of the Scriptures; but it is orthodoxy to say that unless some one or other of these interpretations be implicitly adopted, the Scriptures themselves will profit us nothing.

I call a State " Christian " when it declares its belief in

[a] [For his later feeling on this point, see chap. x. of Life and Correspondence, vol. ii. p. 278. 4th edition.]

the divine origin and supreme authority of the Christian Revelation as contained in the Scriptures; I call this United Kingdom, as yet, a Christian nation, although it be neither Episcopal nor Presbyterian, but establishes the one form in England, and the other in Scotland. I call Prussia a Christian nation, although it be neither Roman Catholic nor Protestant, but establishes the one form of Christianity in Westphalia, and the other in Brandenburg. In such cases there is no difficulty; the nation belongs to the Church of Christ; one part of it under one form, and another under another; and where the followers of these several forms are locally distinct from each other, the State may conveniently allow to each the management of their own concerns in all subordinate matters, only taking care that neither party encroaches upon the other, and neither presumes to excite ill-will against the other. But if either complain that the State is not fit to legislate for them because its supreme government consists indifferently of men of both parties, this supposes so strong a sense of the differences between them, as to render it proper that they should rather form a confederacy than a State. Neighbourhood and mutual interest may fit them for such a relation; but they differ too widely to be united together in so close a connexion as that of fellow-citizens.

Suppose, however, a far more complicated case:—that one particular form of Christianity is established over a whole country, and that this at first is the form adopted by a very great majority of the inhabitants; suppose that afterwards, from various causes, a large proportion of the people object to this form, and set up for themselves others of which they approve more fully; supposing that none of these different forms are locally distinct from one another, but that all exist side by side in the same district, and parish, and town, and street. What is to be done under these circumstances? Are the dissenters from the establishment to be excluded from the legislature, or are they to legislate for a communion to which they themselves do not belong? or, thirdly, may the concerns of the establishment be now safely left to the care of those alone who happen to be members of it?

1. Dissenters need not be excluded from the legislature; for, to speak generally, the differences between Christians are not on such great points of principle or practice as to hinder them from taking the same estimate of the great business of human life, and so to unfit them from walking through it as companions to each other. Their paths are one in the main, both for time and eternity; so that they may well be united with each other in political society. Yet still, if the dissenters be a small minority, and the members of the establishment conscientiously believe that the full rights of citizenship cannot be granted to them; although their exclusion may be unwise, and betray a narrow and unsocial spirit, yet it may not be called unjust. The right of society to judge for itself in such a case cannot be questioned; and individuals can plead no political rights in opposition to society. But the case is wholly altered when, instead of a small minority, they become a substantive part of the whole nation, in numbers, in wealth, and in intelligence and moral qualifications,—it is then no longer society on one side and a few individuals on the other, but society divided against itself, neither part may deny to the other its portion in their common country. The political importance of dissenters, then, under these circumstances, makes it unjust, as well as inexpedient, to exclude them from the legislature.

2. The concerns of the establishment may not safely be left to the exclusive care of its own members. Points of detail may indeed be left to them; nor can any one exactly define how far their own municipal government may be allowed to carry its powers. But the religious establishment being a national concern, the sovereign power can never be justified in abandoning it entirely to private management. Dissent is an evil, and the condition of dissenters is one of disadvantage. The sovereign power, then, as watching over the good of the whole society, should never lose sight of the desirableness of lessening the amount of dissent, if it cannot hope altogether to extinguish it. While fully aware that the separation may prove to be quite as much owing to the dissenters as to the establishment, the government will yet recollect that it becomes the establishment, as holding the vantage ground, to make the first overtures; it is bound to see, not only that no new tests of doctrine or discipline be introduced, which might well be, if the members of the establishment were left sole managers of its affairs,—but also that the existing tests be removed from time to time, so far as may seem expedient, in order to try whether the dissenters would meet such advances in a friendly spirit or no. In short, being trustee, for the nation's benefit, of the immense advantages of a national establishment, it may not make over its trust to other hands who cannot be equally responsible for the due administration of it.

3. Dissenters may legislate for a communion to which they themselves do not belong. They may do so on the ground already assumed, that there is nothing to hinder them from being fellow-citizens with the members of the establishment in the same Christian kingdom. If it be objected that members of the establishment do

not legislate upon the concerns of dissenters, it should be remembered that the cases are not parallel; that the dissenting societies are of a private nature, and therefore are naturally not so subject to the State's control as a society essentially public and national. Private houses are not subject to the same superintendence of the magistrates as those which are open to the public. A man may load his own carriage as he will, but let him set up a conveyance for passengers in general, and the law immediately interferes with his arrangements, and prescribes minutely what number he may carry, and how they are to be distributed.

III. "But the Church is essentially distinct from the State, and ought not to be confounded with it. It may be correct to say that they are allied together, but not that the State is actually the Church." This objection has been brought forward against a former statement of mine by Mr. Dickenson[a], and it is urged with an ability, a fairness, and a courtesy, which cannot but deprive controversy of all its unkindness. I may be allowed to notice his arguments in detail.

The difference between us seems to consist in this; that Mr. Dickenson conceives of the ideas of State and Church as expressing societies whose objects are *essentially* distinct, while I regard the distinction as only *accidental.* No doubt a man who thinks with Warburton, that the sole object of political society is "the conservation of body and goods," must regard the distinction between Church and State as necessary and perpetual; so must those also who think that the proper object of the Church is to keep up in their purity the ritual ordinances of religion, ($\theta\rho\eta\sigma\kappa\epsilon\iota\alpha,$) such as public prayer, sacrifices, and the like. Now

[a] [The late Bishop of Meath.]

as we have seen above, that States, in practice, have very often confined their attention to the physical welfare of society; and as the greater number of religious societies or institutions have really been appointed for ritual services, it is not surprising that the objects of each should have been very often estimated unworthily. But define the object of the Church to be what Warburton calls it, " the advancement and improvement of our intellectual nature,"[a] and it becomes as nearly as possible identical with what Aristotle declares to be the object of the State, namely, the happiness of society; happiness, as he expressly insists, consisting both in physical and moral good, but much more in the latter than in the former[b]. Now every State not being Christian seeks man's highest happiness with mistaken views; its pursuit of the true object is not according to knowledge; and every Church, before the State becomes Christian, seeks man's highest happiness, since the cessation of miraculous gifts, with deficient power. It is constantly thwarted by not possessing the sovereign control over human life, the power of outward dominion. But the State is capable of receiving the knowledge of the Church, whereas it cannot part with its essential attribute of sovereignty, nor is the Church fitted to exercise it. Thus the State[c] having been enlightened by the knowledge of the Church, becomes a society seeking the same end which the Church sought, and with the same knowledge, but with

[a] The first object of religion, he observes, is to procure the favour of God; but for this object man had no occasion to constitute a society. The second object of *religion* is the first object of *religious society*, namely, the advancement and improvement of our intellectual nature. (*Warburton, Alliance of Church and State,* book i. chap. 5.)

[b] Aristotle, Politics, i. 1, vii. 1, 2, 3. 13.

[c] [See Postscript to Principles of Church Reform.]

more extensive outward means of attaining it, because its inherent sovereignty gives it a greater power over outward things. And this was my meaning when I said that, in a country where the nation and government are avowedly and essentially Christian, the State or nation was virtually the Church.

I am not quite sure that the expression " national universities" is generally applied to Oxford and Cambridge. But suppose that the whole education of the country were conducted by law upon one system; that the smaller schools were placed under the control of the larger, and these again under the government of the Universities, this grand society for the purposes of education might certainly be called " national," or belonging to the nation, but it could not be *identified with the nation*, for this reason, that the object of such a society would be subordinate to that of the nation or State, and distinct from it, being limited to " the good education of the young." And further[a], all the members of the State would not be members of this particular society, but only those who were either educating others, or being educated themselves. And so of all other societies or institutions employed by the State, whose ends or objects are conducive to the object of the state, but subordinate to it, and only fulfilling a certain part of it.

So far my statement as to the identity of the State and Church under certain circumstances may be intelligible, perhaps, whatever opinion be entertained of its truth and falsehood. But what becomes of this view where there exist within the same State different forms of Christianity, and still more when two forms are actually established at the same time in different

---

a | See Sermons, vol. iv. p. 413.]

parts of the same kingdom, as in England and Scotland? How can the State be at the same time identical with two different Churches, with the Kirk of Scotland, and with the Church of England?

This will be a formidable objection to those who think that the essential character of Christ's Church is to be found in the peculiarities of any one particular denomination of Christians. But if these peculiarities are not essential, and if both the Church of England and the Kirk of Scotland are equally members of Christ's Church, then it is very possible for the State to be virtually the Church of Christ in those countries subject to its dominion, but yet to allow its members to adopt such particular rites and such a peculiar municipal government in different places as they may respectively judge convenient. And this is no more than exists continually in civil matters; different provinces and towns of the same State having frequently different customs and different municipal privileges, all of which the State acknowledges and authorizes, without feeling its own essential unity impaired by such varieties.

This also is agreeable to the notion implied in that expression at which some are so fond of cavilling; " that Christianity is part and parcel of the law of the land." It is not pretended that " Christianity" means here " any particular form of Christianity," and, therefore attacks on the peculiar doctrines and discipline of the Church of England are not illegal; but attacks on the truth of Christianity in general are. I am not impugning or defending the propriety of the laws against blasphemy; I am merely noticing the distinction made between Christianity and any one particular form of it; and showing that the State may be Christian, and yet may sanction or even establish within its dominions many particular societies of Christians, that is, in another and subordinate sense *many different Churches* —though all in the higher sense to the term belong to *one and the same Church*,—that Church with which I have said that every Christian State is within its own dominions virtually identical.

And now I am come to consider that other great error with respect to the Church, which has so eternally embroiled the whole question; which has led men to talk of the alliance between Church and State in some instances, and absolutely to deny the sovereignty of the State in others; an error, however, which has produced far more and worse effects than these, having done more lasting injury to Christianity than any other perhaps which can be named. For, by a happy fertility in evil, it has suited the bad tendencies of two opposite descriptions of characters,—encouraging on the one hand superstition, fraud, uncharitableness and tyranny, and on the other hand leading to a general carelessness of principle, to profaneness and all licentiousness. This error is the confounding the Christian clergy with the hereditary priesthoods of Judaism and Heathenism; and thus conceiving of the clergy as of an order preserving its identity by perpetual succession, and being invested with certain indefeasible powers, which were neither derived from human authority, and which no human law can modify or take away. And the consideration of this grand error shall form the second part of the present discussion.

CHAPTER II.

When Cyrus seated himself on the throne of the kings of Media, the Magians, who composed the Median priesthood, were left in undisturbed possession of their sacred dignity. The king was from henceforth a Persian, and Persians naturally filled the principal military offices of the empire; but the priesthood was still confined to the Medes, and in religious matters their conquerors submitted to their discipline. Now this arrangement may be called with very little impropriety a real alliance between the State and the Church. The parties were in the outset independent of one another, the Magians not being the natural subjects of Cyrus; they were distinguished from one another by difference of race, and each stood in need of the other's co-operation; the Magians could not have resisted the sword of the conqueror, while he on his side found his Persian countrymen too ignorant to form a priesthood themselves, and hoped, besides, to conciliate his new subjects by preserving the sacred character of that order whom they had been so long accustomed to venerate.

Now when the German chiefs established themselves and their followers in the various provinces of the Roman empire, they treated the Christian clergy in many instances just as Cyrus had treated the Magians. Their own countrymen were visibly inferior in knowledge, whilst the Roman clergy had long been respected and loved by their people, and this influence might be made useful to the authority of the new sovereign. It may be said that here also there was an alliance between Church and State, which has subsisted ever since in virtue of this beginning.

Let us now observe the essential differences between these two transactions, apparently so similar. In the case of the Magians, as of the other priesthoods of antiquity, they constituted by themselves the whole of the religious society with which the conqueror allied himself; the people were never supposed to constitute a part of it. Again, the chief religious office was sacrifice, which could not be performed acceptably to the gods, unless by a priest; and, therefore, as the priesthood was hereditary, there was an essential act of religion inseparably connected with the Magians, which could be performed by none but themselves and their posterity. They thus possessed an unalienable property, so that it was worth the State's while to enter into a perpetual alliance with them, because the benefits derived from them were such as could at no future time be enjoyed unless through their instrumentality.

But in the case of the Roman clergy, they were not the Church, nor was any bargain formed with them for their advancement in wealth or dignity entitled to be called a covenant made with the Church. Nor, again, did they possess any unalienable and peculiar power, essential to the perfection of Christianity, so that their services would at all future times be indispensable to the State, and could be supplied from no other quarter. Their knowledge, when once communicated, passed to the disciple in all the perfection in which it was enjoyed by the teacher, and the disciple could in the same way impart it to others. In such cases the original communicator of any knowledge may be remunerated by a certain definite reward, or may be invested with certain privileges for a limited term of years; but the State encroaches on the just sovereignty of future generations, if it confers a perpetual monopoly of any important office, which, after a lapse of years, may be filled as well by other citizens as by those who are thus put in exclusive possession of it.

It will not be improper to observe that the clergy, as if aware of this, laboured actually to represent themselves as standing in a position different from this real one. Language was so far abused, that "the Church," in common speech, was generally understood to mean "the clergy;" the "honour and welfare of the Church" meant no more than the "advancement and enrichment of the clergy." They also called themselves "priests," and, consistently with the name, professed that they were empowered and exclusively commissioned to offer sacrifice for the people, and to forgive their sins. And thus they tried to put themselves in the place of the ancient hereditary priesthoods, and to make *their order*, as distinguished from their knowledge, essential in all times alike to the perfect developement of Christianity.

In short, all the arguments about the alliance of the Church with the State, its inherent independence, &c., &c., rest upon this supposition,—that the Church has certain governors unalterably defined by God himself, and that these governors possess certain inherent and essential powers which can only be communicated through their medium; in short, that Christianity has its priesthood, like other religions, invested with an indefeasible personal sacredness and authority.

The institutions, the writings, the practice, and the language of Christian Europe, for several centuries, have assumed this supposition to be true; not that in all cases it has been distinctly avowed, or even perceived, for then its falsehood would long ago have been detected; but it has been implied, and tacitly taken for granted. And yet never was there a notion more unsupported by any shadow of reason or of authority;

never was there an error more deeply mischievous.

But here, as in other matters, this justice must be done to the Roman Catholics, that they have at least been consistent in their error. Their system is intelligible and harmonious; its symmetry is perfect, and its reasonableness would be unanswerable, if it were based upon a true foundation. It was reserved, not certainly for the Church of England in its official acts, but for a powerful party of its individual members, to exhibit a far more melancholy proof of the perversity of the human mind. For these persons, while maintaining the erroneous conclusions of the Roman Catholics, have at the same time denied the foundation from which alone they could be legitimately derived; betraying a mind not only unstartled by a false opinion, but incapable of examining the reasons on which it might claim to be received; not only maintaining an absurdity, but maintaining it in contradiction to principles which itself avowed.

Before I enter, however, upon the question itself, there is one distinction most important to a right understanding of my argument, which I am anxious to impress deeply on my readers' minds: I am contending not against any office or institution in itself, but against a foolish, presumptuous, and schismatical claim set up by some of its weak or furious admirers. I am very far from arguing against episcopal government; on the contrary, I have recorded my earnest wish that it may [a] become more generally received, and more effectually enforced. But I am arguing against its being made an essential point in Christianity;— against the manifold confusions and superstitions, and

[a] [Principles of Church Reform.]

insolent uncharitablenesses with which its cause has been embarrassed; against the mischiefs which threaten the Church of England from the outcry set up about the profanation of secular interference with sacred things. I am maintaining the self-same argument against the High Church superstition of the present day, which Hooker upheld, in his time, against the superstition of the Puritans, namely, the sovereignty of the Christian State over all its subordinate offices, whether ecclesiastical or civil. Or to appeal to a still higher authority, the argument here insisted on, and the calumnies to which it subjects its advocates, are precisely similar to the course followed by St. Paul with respect to the Jewish Law, and to the slanders and malignity with which the Judaizing Christians, the High Churchmen of those days, assailed him in consequence of it. For while he himself " walked orderly and kept the Law," while he even circumcised Timothy in order to conciliate, as far as he honestly could, the prejudices of the Jews, he was accused by the zealots of " teaching all the Jews to forsake Moses, saying that they ought not to circumcise their children, nor to keep their customs." But the falsehood had this foundation in truth, that St. Paul had struggled most earnestly against the unchristian pretension, " that the Law of Moses was an essential part of Christ's Gospel." It was not only harmless, but becoming to the Jewish Christians, so long as they observed it as a venerable institution handed down to them from their forefathers; and formerly, under different circumstances, commanded by God himself. But it became injurious, nay, subversive of the souls of men, when it was put forward as necessary to salvation, and attempted, in the spirit of fanaticism or worldly ambition, to be forced upon the acceptance of all Christians. Nor could St.

Paul forbear the language of the strongest condemnation when these Judaizers attempted to shake the lawful government of the Christian Church, because it had interfered with their selfishness and superstition. They disputed St. Paul's Apostleship as irregular, because he had not, like Matthias, received his appointment through the medium of the original Apostles of Christ; because, in defence of the essential liberty of Christ's Gospel, he had resisted the highest human authority, and reproved even Peter himself. Such is ever the nature of superstition,—anarchical at once and tyrannical; virulent in proportion to its ignorance, and lax in matters of principle consistently with its intolerant strictness on points of form. Such is that spirit which, incapable of comprehending the pure and loving bond of Christian union, spares no pains and scruples at no means to make proselytes to its own paltry party; and on which our Lord Himself,—who, in true zeal for God's service, as in every thing else, is alone our perfect pattern,—has pronounced one of His heaviest sentences of condemnation.

First, then, let us see how much is implied in the undeniable truth, that Christianity acknowledges no earthly priesthood. People have no objection, at least in Protestant countries, to allow this as a fact, because they think that it means no more than that the practice of offering sacrifices is done away. But the particular rite of sacrifice seems to have been only an accident of the priestly character, although it is the best example of what was conceived essential to it. The proper notion of a priest is of a mediator between God and man, of one who, being purer and nearer to the object of his worship than other men, is the only medium through whom other men may communicate with their God. The notion of " teaching religion " is by no means a part of the priestly office, except so far as regards the enforcing of an exact observance of external rites. For he who teaches another religion in the higher sense, teaches him how he may please God by himself; whereas a priesthood supposes that a man cannot please God by himself, but requires another man to present his prayers and his worship for him, because he is himself unclean. Thus a priesthood implies an abiding superiority of one man or set of men over another in their relations to God; such a superiority, in fact, as argues a distinction of race; and therefore it was natural that no person of another race should be thought capable of holding it without pollution. This was the reason why it was so generally hereditary, and a similar reason led to the establishment of the principle of hereditary succession in the monarchies of antiquity; the kings being supposed to belong to a nobler and higher race than those over whom they ruled. But where the monarchy was the creation of a later age, and was connected with no heroic or divine founder, as in the case of the Roman imperial government, there the throne was not necessarily hereditary, and could never be claimed simply by right of descent[a].

The priesthood amongst the Israelites, being there

---

[a] The monarchies of modern Europe became hereditary, not as offices, but as property: the king's son succeeded to his father's kingdom as to an estate, the possession of which involved, no doubt, certain duties towards the tenants or vassals who lived on it, but was obtained by no rule of political fitness, simply on the notion of inheritance. This is particularly shown in those countries where females are capable of succeeding to the crown; an exception to the universal rule in all other cases, if the royalty had been looked upon as the highest magistracy in the State, but regular and natural if it were regarded as an inheritance of property, which, like other properties naturally invested its owner with jurisdiction over those who lived on it.

ingrafted upon the true religion, presented undoubtedly some peculiar features. There the priests were known to be of the same origin with the rest of the people, nor were they supposed to be morally superior to them. But the Israelitish Religion required sacrifices, and a priesthood, as typical of the great sacrifice to be made by the true High Priest hereafter. Such peculiarities, therefore, of the priestly character were to be retained as should show that there was a real priesthood, according to the common notions entertained of the term, and yet should not interfere with the moral improvement of the people. A sort of ceremonial purity was attached to the priest, and his sacrifices were to procure an outward and ceremonial atonement. Thus far the race of Aaron were set apart from their brethren; thus far they were more holy than other men, and accordingly the priesthood was confined to them exclusively. It may be observed, also, that the constant succession of prophets, chosen from any tribe or family without distinction, from the lowest classes, as in the case of Amos, no less than the highest, and invested with a power over the concerns of life far greater [a] than that of the priests, was a continual intimation that the instruction and improvement of the people in the great end of religion, holiness of heart, has no necessary connexion with an hereditary priesthood.

To return, however, to general history: as experience disproves the perpetual moral superiority of one family or race over others; nay, as it is found that a race which carefully avoids all mixture with others, is, from that very cause, apt to degenerate, so an order of priests at first strictly hereditary might be inclined to

---

[a] [See Sermons, vol. vi.; "The Disobedient Prophet."]

rest their power, in the course of time, on a more real superiority, by retaining to themselves the possession of superior knowledge. For this end it would be desirable to strengthen their body by the accession of individuals of other races whose talents or dispositions might make them useful auxiliaries, and who, being trained in their discipline, became, in fact, the adopted children of their race. Such was the system pursued by the Druids; their order was frequently swelled by the accession of young men who were not Druids by birth, but who were brought up in their schools, and admitted by them afterwards to share their power and privileges. But this was only a more effectual means of securing the essence of a priesthood, a superiority over the rest of the people. The Druids were very careful in teaching those who were to become Druids themselves, but they were as careful that the superior knowledge of their order should not be communicated to any who were without their pale; and with this view they made their instruction wholly verbal, no part of their knowledge was committed to writing. There was a reason, then, why they should constitute a distinct order, and why they alone should have the power of appointing those who were to be admitted to it, because by keeping their knowledge within their own custody they insured to themselves a perpetual superiority.

Thus there appears a perpetual connexion between the notion of a priesthood and that of an order either absolutely hereditary, or possessing the exclusive right of appointing its own members. And this is further confirmed by the fact, that the Christian clergy, while they claimed the privileges of a priesthood, did, in fact, endeavour to show that they possessed also the inherent superiority of a priesthood. They made their order synonymous[a] with the whole Church, as if, after the example of the heathen priesthoods, none but themselves were fit members of a religious society; they pretended that Christianity still retained the rite of sacrifice, which implied of necessity a priest to offer it; and in order to make their superiority real, they recruited themselves from all races and ranks of men indiscriminately, but were careful that the knowledge of religion should be as much as possible confined to themselves: and whereas this had been committed to writing already, and the written document might not be destroyed, still they trod in the steps of the Druids as nearly as they could, by preventing the people from getting access to it, and by setting up a vast mass of oral traditions, said to have been handed down amongst themselves, which they pretended were of equal authority.

What has been thus far said will excite a strong presumption that the claims of the Christian clergy to exist as a distinct order, with the exclusive right of admitting new members to their own body, and with powers and privileges not derived from any human law, have been grounded on the mistaken notion of their being a priesthood; because such claims do flow naturally from the essential notion of a priesthood, and have not been commonly made or allowed in other cases where no such notion has existed. It is very true that those Protestants of the Church of England, who, whilst allowing that they are not priests, wish to claim the privileges of a priesthood, are obliged to rest their claim upon a different ground; but assertions made and admitted in the first instance upon grounds which will not bear inquiry, are often defended afterwards upon other princi-

---

[a] [See Appendix I. to Sermons, vol. iii.]

ples; principles too inconclusive to have ever established the conclusion originally, but which are fitted for the far easier office of inducing men to remain in that conclusion, when their habits and institutions have already been formed upon it. These afterthoughts, it must be confessed, are very apt to betray the urgent necessity which drove men to have recourse to them; they are arguments which none would ever have employed if they could have helped it. The ground then assumed by these Protestants who wish to keep the conclusions of the Roman Catholics after they have denied their premises, seems to be this, so far as it is possible to understand it—that the clergy derive their power by succession from the Apostles, and that they having the exclusive right of administering the Sacraments, and the Sacraments being essential to Christianity, so a clergy, as it is called, of pure apostolical descent, can never be dispensed with in the Christian Church, and that where there is no such clergy, then there is no part of Christ's Church.

I must again remind the reader that the question in no degree turns upon the propriety or impropriety of the clergy possessing such and such powers, but simply upon the tenure by which they hold them. Nothing can be more proper than that the Sacraments should be administered by a regularly appointed ministry; nothing less to be desired than any alteration of the ordinances of the Church of England in these points. But are these ministers the officers of the Church, and appointed by its supreme government, or are they not its officers but its priests, and deriving their appointment, not from it nor its sanction, but from the purity of their spiritual descent? The question is evidently most important, inasmuch as it touches the question, whether the Church is or is not sovereign over all its members, or whether there are some who are not its members, but its hereditary masters.

When it is said that the clergy "derive their authority from their apostolical descent," I should like to know what is meant by the words. Is it meant that this apostolical descent conveys to them any real intrinsic gift, moral or intellectual, so that they may claim the power of priests, because they possess a real superiority over other men, or a higher degree of knowledge? Or is it meant that they are not a priesthood but an oligarchy, and that the Apostles fixed invariably the form of the government of the Church throughout all ages, without giving it withal any portion of that real virtue, which can alone render forms other than essentially[a] indifferent and changeable? Was the object, in short, of this supposed apostolical institution spiritual or political?

Again, when "the authority of the clergy" is spoken of, is it meant that this authority is absolute, or where is the power of limiting it? It is intelligible enough certainly, if the position maintained is this,—that the bishops as supreme, and the other clergy as their subordinate officers, have sovereign power over the Christian Church in all ages, independent of any human law: that they may alone fill up the vacancies in their own body, or may increase and diminish its numbers at their pleasure; that they may legislate for the Church as to doctrine, morals, and ritual, and punish disobedience to their laws by excommunication; that as no society can exist without something of a public purse or revenue, they may determine the amount of this revenue and the manner of its application: and, finally, that if they abuse their power the Church is without

[a] [See "The Christian Duty of Conceding the Roman Catholic Claims."]

remedy, as they are amenable to none but God for its exercise. This is intelligible, but I much doubt whether any one will be found hardy enough to assert it. But if the authority of the bishops and clergy be limited, where are we to find its limits: are they fixed or variable? and who has the power of enforcing them? If the Church has a constitution, where are we to look for its provisions? Was it given complete at once by Divine authority, or has it been the gradual work of the Church itself in different ages, and therefore alterable by the same authority which enacted it? Or if partly divine and partly human, how are we to distinguish exactly between the one and the other? Above all, where is the sovereignty of the Church vested? that supreme power which must exist somewhere in every society, and by which all the concerns of the society are in the last resort regulated?

It would be well if those persons who venture to talk of the legislature committing " a dangerous infringement on the rights of the Church by remodelling the dioceses of Ireland" would attempt to answer these questions, and to show that they have some little understanding of matters of law and government, before they allow themselves to use language which is little less than seditious. Is it Christian conduct to endeavour to excite weak though well-meaning persons against the supreme government of their country, by repeating to them a string of idle phrases about apostolical succession, without any definite notion of the meaning of the very words which they are echoing? One writer[a], who, it seems, is very anxious to circulate

---

[a] [This and much of the argument in connexion with it, has reference to the temporary controversy with the Oxford Tracts for the Times, especially No. 7 of the series, published October 29, 1833. See Introd. to Serm. vol. iv. p. 19.]

his instructions as widely as possible, talks of our present bishops being "the heirs and representatives of the Apostles," and of having "the gifts of ruling and ordaining, of teaching, of binding and loosing." It is the most painful circumstance attending such foolish writing about the most sacred subjects, that, whilst putting it down as it deserves, we may be exposed to the charge of irreverence towards the high and holy things themselves which it has dared to profane. But is it the way to give any definite notion of the extent and dignity of the episcopal office in the Church of England, to say that the bishops are "the heirs and representatives of the Apostles?" Heirs and representatives to what, and in what? Does it mean heirs of their power,—so that the bishops may and can do all that the Apostles did? Or if it means "heirs of a portion of their power,"—will the writer tell us of what and of how large a portion, and by what authority it was or is defined? Again, "representatives of the Apostles" in what? Does he mean in all points? or if not, will he specify in what? The bishops have "the gifts of ruling and ordaining, of teaching, of binding, and loosing." Does he mean that they are *authorized* to exercise these functions, or *qualified to exercise them well?* The gifts of the Holy Spirit, spoken of in the Scripture, are certain enlargements of men's natural powers in order to enable them to do their several works in the Church more effectually: thus, the "gift of teaching" would signify "the gift of such knowledge and such powers of communicating it, as would make a man a good teacher." Does he mean that all our clergy possess such a gift of teaching? or, if by "the gift of ruling" he means only "authority to rule," then what is meant by the term "ruling"? Is it absolute rule, or limited? and if limited, how far and by what authority? Again, with respect to "the gift of binding and loosing." Does he mean that the bishops can forgive sins or refuse forgiveness? that they can declare with God's authority what things are lawful to be done by Christians, and what are unlawful? These are the two senses in which the terms "binding and loosing" are to be understood, where they occur in the Scriptures; and in both of these the Apostles had power to bind and to loose. Is it in these senses, or in either of them, that the terms are to be understood when applied to our present bishops?

I have said that superstition is anarchical; and the language of the writer whom I have been quoting is a good example of this. He seems to think that if it were not for what he calls their apostolical succession, the clergy would have no authority to speak to the people in the name of Christ. Has the king no authority to rule; nay, does he not most truly rule by a divine right, because he derives his power from the law? So every man appointed by the law to minister in the Church, ministers by divine authority; the voice of the law is as the voice of God. Not that the law could make a man a *priest*, that is, it could neither give him superior purity nor superior knowledge, it could communicate no inherent personal virtue. But the law can make a *minister*, that is, can qualify a man legally to exercise those functions which naturally and personally any other member of the Church may be equally fitted to discharge; for it should be always remembered that the knowledge required for the ministerial office has been entrusted not to any one peculiar order of men, but to the whole Church; the minister takes of the knowledge thus committed to the society of believers, and communicates it to such individual believers as may stand in need of it; but with respect to the Church at large he is not a teacher, but a minister—he can tell the church nothing more than it knows already—he is in possession of no mystery or secret of godliness which has not been imparted long since to all believers; and, therefore, the law of the Church may fitly appoint him to his ministerial office, and remove him from it; just as the law of the state in any heathen country may appoint its magistrates, its generals, or its professors of science and philosophy, because all these, though by possibility superior in the knowledge of their respective callings to every other individual in the state, have yet only availed themselves of that which lay equally open to other men, and which the state, therefore, considered in the abstract, may be considered to possess as well as they.

Let us here observe again the consistency and sagacity of the Roman Catholics in adapting their several doctrines to one another. Their notion of apostolical succession is accompanied by their belief in apostolical tradition. Thus according to them there is a knowledge entrusted to the successors of the apostles, which is not accessible but through their medium; the written word of God is not complete without the addition of the unwritten. The Roman Catholics then may call their ministry a priesthood without inconsistency, because they maintain that it was made the exclusive depository of a part of the knowledge of God's will.

But the fundamental truth of Protestantism, that God's revealed will is known to us only through the Scriptures, deprives the Protestant supporters of apostolical succession of the best justification of their belief. Shut out then from this reasonable argument, their resource, like that of some pretended philosophers of old, is in obscurity, and in assertions which relating to matters without the range of human knowledge, can neither be proved nor disproved. For when they say that the efficacy of the sacraments depends on the apostolical descent of those who administer them, the subject being altogether beyond our understanding, we cannot positively say that the assertion is false, but we are sure that it is most presumptuous, inasmuch as there are no grounds whatever for believing it to be true. It is just such another assertion as the Romish doctrine of Transubstantiation; which is not, as many suppose, a mere absurdity, but a statement about matters wholly incomprehensible; for when it is said that all which we know of bread is still left in the consecrated wafer, that is, its appearance, taste, smell, &c., but that the substance of bread is gone, and is succeeded by another substance, of which no faculty either of our body or mind can take cognizance; such a doctrine is not so certainly false in itself, as it implies the fondest presumption and folly in those who gratuitously maintain it. So with regard to the virtue of Christ's ordinance depending on the apostolical descent of its ministers, we can certainly say that such a doctrine has not been taught us by Christ or His Apostles; that it is inconsistent with the character of Christ's gospel, and gives occasion to many superstitions; and that as we have no reason whatever for believing it to be true, so its practical evil tendency justifies us in acting with regard to it as if it were certainly false.

Let not this fantastical and superstitious notion be confounded with the reasonable and reverent ordinance of the Church of England, that the sacraments should be generally administered by none but her appointed ministers. As a matter of order, propriety, and solemnity, nothing can be determined more wisely; but the whole question at issue is, whether these ministers have any authority or any inherent qualification for the administration of the sacraments independently of her appointment. In other words, whether the nonjuring clergy after their deprivation had any spiritual qualification to act as ministers; whether they did not become laymen by divine law as well as by the law of the land, until some particular Church or congregation of Christians should have again called them to the ministry. And, on the other hand, supposing the story of the Nag's Head Consecration of Archbishop Parker to have been true, whether he would not have been as truly an archbishop by divine right, and a genuine successor of the apostles, so far as any Christian minister can now be so, by virtue of his appointment from the supreme government of this Church of England.

Hitherto I have treated the question on general grounds. I have shown that as the Christian ministry are not a priesthood, as they neither possess nor can transmit any personal superiority, whether of holiness or of knowledge, there can be conceived no reason why they should constitute an exception to the general rule of all society; that the form of its government is fixed by law, a law in its origin framed by man, but becoming in its power of requiring obedience the law of God, because God in such matters, having given no express ordinance of his own by revelation, has vouchsafed his sanction to the ordinances of society, to prevent the mischiefs of individual lawlessness. Now the weakness of superstition has in this matter always served the cause of licentious wickedness. For it being its nature always to "desire a sign," to look for God in the whirlwind or in the earthquake or in the fire, it is slow to recognise the still small voice of His providence or of His Spirit; it complains, therefore, of the insufficient authority of law, and refuses its obedience to it, professing to follow an immediate direction from heaven. And wickedness, seeing it thus busied in undermining what is really of Divine authority, cares little for the phantom which it would introduce in its room; well knowing that such phantoms never hinder its own success, but most times greatly further it, by furnishing the better part of human nature with that which cannot nourish or strengthen it, yet by its fair show prevents it from seeking the true bread of life elsewhere, and so leaving the evil unchecked to take its own course, and to work greedily all manner of iniquity, and of uncleanness, and of uncharitableness, and of ungodliness.

This general view of the nature of law and government is also essential towards a right understanding of those particular texts of Scripture to which an appeal has so often been made by the disputants on both sides of the question. And the High Churchmen of the present day, like the Puritan antagonists of Hooker, disregarding such general views altogether, are not aware of the difficulties, inconsistencies, and extravagances into which their interpretation of these texts involves them; nor are they less misled by their ignorance of the true way of applying the lessons of history. They appeal to the practice of the early Christian Churches as confirming their view of the divine authority of Episcopacy; whereas, even admitting the decisions of the early Christians to be our standard, their practice could but show the lawfulness of Episcopacy, not its indispensable necessity. Till the growth of the Italian republics, in the middle ages, Christians had, with hardly a single exception, lived from the beginning of the Gospel under monarchical governments. Is this an argument that no other form is consistent with Christianity? And it is worth observing, that the zealots for monarchy in the sixteenth and seventeenth centuries did plead its great antiquity and its universality in the earliest period of history, as reasons for preferring it to all other forms. History, according to the well-known saying, is philosophy teaching by examples; but the apparent easiness of such a manner of teaching has hindered men from profiting by it. They appeal to examples before they understand on what the force of an example depends. Now as much of the most important part of history has been neglected by common historians, the knowledge of the accompanying circumstances under which any institution existed is not to be obtained without some research, and some power of historical divination; that is, a power of filling up the fragments of direct information, which are often all that we can obtain; just as Cuvier's profound knowledge of comparative anatomy enabled him to divine the whole structure and habits of an extinct species of animals from the study of a single bone of any individual of it. Thus the simple fact of the existence of Episcopacy amongst the early Christians is pleaded as an example for Christians now, whereas it is, in fact, no example at all; first, because it remains to be proved whether so much of the institution as it is proposed to perpetuate was its essence, or only an accidental adjunct; secondly, because the circumstances of the two cases are different, and there are reasons why Episcopacy should have been universally adopted, *de facto*, then, which by no means prove that it must be adopted, *de jure*, now and for ever.

I now propose to examine what support or countenance is given by the Scriptures to the positions of the English High Churchmen, namely, that the Church ought always, and in all countries, to be governed by bishops, priests, and deacons; that these ministers derive their authority from their apostolical descent;

that of these, bishops only may ordain other ministers, and bishops and priests may alone administer both the Sacraments; that where this succession is duly kept up, there the Church retains its identity, and is a true Church; where it is interrupted or neglected, there the Church loses its title to the name; and that without the concurrence of the successors of the Apostles, or the majority of them, no alteration can lawfully be made, either in Church discipline or doctrine. Let it be once again repeated, that the question is not about the lawfulness or expediency in any particular case of a system such as is here supposed, but about its necessity; not whether Episcopacy be the best form of government which any Church can establish, but whether it be unlawful to establish any other; and whether its powers have been so clearly defined by Christ and his Apostles as to leave the Church no right of interference to modify or to limit them.

First, it is, I think, undeniable, that the general tone of the New Testament strongly discountenances the notion of an inherent purity, or knowledge, or authority, existing in any one order of the Christian Church, as distinguished from the rest. Nothing can be more adverse to the claims of a priesthood than our Lord's charge to His disciples,—" Be not ye called Rabbi, for one is your master, even Christ; and all ye are brethren." (Matt. xxiii. 8.) The obvious meaning of these words, especially when taken with the context, is to condemn the pretension of any Christian to teach his brethren with *authority*. He might teach them so far as his understanding or knowledge were superior to theirs, but no further. And to the same purpose are the words of Jeremiah, especially quoted in the Epistle to the Hebrews, (viii. 11,) as characterizing the Christian dispensation,—" And they shall not teach every man his neighbour and every man his brother, saying, Know the Lord: for all shall know me from the least to the greatest." It seems to me that this passage shows that an order of men set apart to teach their brethren is no essential and eternal part of the plan of Christianity. A ministry varying in its constitution and powers according to the wants of the Church, at various periods, is only a help towards the attainment of this perfect state; but a priesthood transmitted by succession, and endowed with powers indefeasible, would imply that no such state was to be aimed at; that it was a part of the original design of the Christian Religion, no less than that of Moses, that man should never draw near to God but through the mediation or assistance of another man. Again, the story of the man (Mark ix. 38, Luke ix. 49.) who cast out devils in Christ's name, but was not one of His company, speaks as strongly as any thing can speak, against insisting on the necessity of any point of outward form. The language of the disciples, " Master, we saw one casting out devils in thy name, and we forbade him, because he followeth not with us," has been repeated over and over again in later times, by Christians of various denominations, all alike insisting on their neighbour's agreeing with them, not only in spirit, but in form; whereas Christ's answer blames them for insisting on such matters, as being in their nature wholly indifferent: and if He did not require that all should follow even Himself in outward society, which of His disciples shall dare to say that conformity with them in points of external arrangement is a thing indispensable?

These passages, I allow, show merely the general spirit of Christianity, and of course it would be absurd to argue from them that no individual should submit to another's teaching, or that individuals may despise and disobey all the regulations of the society to which they belong, if they relate only to points of form. But speaking in the mass, they do seem to prove that the Church of Christ is not to be subjected to the authoritative teaching of any of its members, nor to be tied to one model of outward organization. To the same purpose also may be quoted our Lord's directions, as to the course which His disciples were to follow in the case of their private quarrels. The command in the last resort is, " Tell it to the Church, and if he neglect to hear the Church, let him be unto thee as an heathen man and a publican." The Roman Catholics have cut the knot boldly, and say, that " tell it to the Church " means " tell it to the Clergy." It may mean the clergy, wherever the Church has conferred on them the supreme government; but the very use of the general word " Church " seems to show that the society of Christians at large, and not any one order of men amongst them, has the power of determining in every particular age and country whom in practice it is to mean, that is to say, what is to constitute the supreme power in the Church, so that disobedience to it is disobedience to the Church itself, and justly involves exclusion from its communion.

It would have been impossible to suppose, had not experience proved it, that any one could have drawn an argument for the divine right of Episcopacy from our Lord's last charge to His disciples, as recorded by St. Matthew. " And Jesus came and spake unto them, saying, All power is given unto me in heaven and in earth, go ye therefore and teach all nations, baptizing them in the name of the Father, and of the Son, and of the Holy Ghost, teaching them to observe all things whatsoever I have commanded you; and lo, I am with you always, even unto the end of the world."

One would have thought that a charge so solemn and a promise so comforting might have escaped the profanation of sectarian folly. " In one sense," says the writer, whose comment I allude to, " the Apostles were to be alive till He came again; but they all died at the natural time. Does it not follow that there are those now alive who represent them? Now who were the most probable representatives of them in the generation next their death? They surely whom they have ordained to succeed them in the ministerial work. If any persons could be said to have Christ's power and presence, and the gifts of ruling and ordaining, of teaching, of binding and loosing, (and, comparing together the various Scriptures on the subject, all these seem included in his promise to be with the Church always,) surely those on whom the apostles laid their hands were they. And so in the next age, if any were representatives of the first representatives, they must be the next generation of bishops, and so on. *Nor does it materially alter the argument*, though we suppose the blessing upon ministerial offices made, not to the Apostles, but to the whole body of disciples, i. e. the Church. For even if it be the Church that has the power of ordination committed to it, still it exercises it through the bishops as its organs; and the question recurs, how has the presbytery in this or that country obtained the power." I quote the passage at length to show the sort of interpretation and of argument to which those are driven who cling to the conclusions of the Roman Catholics, without retaining the arguments by which the Roman Catholics consistently maintain them. A part of this passage I have already noticed before; now let us consider the general drift of it. The words " I am with you always," refer to the Apostles. For a moment admit that they do, and what follows? "There are some now alive who represent them." Certainly, so far as to be able to apply to themselves in some substantial sense the promise originally made to the Apostles. "And these in the next generation were the persons whom the Apostles ordained." Undoubtedly they might have their interest in Christ's promise, but already in a different sense of the words; for although in many instances, perhaps in all, they had received from the Apostles the " gifts of the Holy Ghost" themselves, i. e. the gift of tongues, or of prophesying and preaching, or of healing, or of working miracles generally, or of knowledge, or of discerning of spirits, (See 1 Corinth. xii. 8-10, 29-30,) yet they had not the power of transmitting these gifts, (Acts viii. 14-17, compare Romans, i. 11,) and therefore the power of Christ was already with them in less measure. " And so in the next age, the representatives must be the next generation of bishops, and so on." In the next age the bishops would not only have lost the power of transmitting the gifts of the Holy Ghost, but they would be without them in their own persons: that extraordinary power of Christ's Spirit, which had been the fit warrant for the extraordinary authority enjoyed by the Apostles, and in a less degree by those on whom they had laid their hands, was now withdrawn, and the claim to extraordinary authority inevitably died with it. From that moment the ordinary principles of all government resumed their exercise; and there being no individuals in the Church whom Christ by His Spirit had Himself in a manner marked out for the ministry, giving them gifts which man could not give, the Church, as a matter of course, became entitled to appoint them herself, because the promises of Christ had now all centered in her, and her gifts were greater than those of her individual members.

Thus the bishops in the third generation from the Apostles were in one sense their successors, as being the chief persons in the Church now, as the Apostles had been in their time; but their power was infinitely diminished, and the tenure by which they held it was necessarily different. " Christ was with them " still, but no longer in the same manner. He was with them as members of His body, He was with them as labouring in His service, and doing His work. And the more solemn and important the work to which they had been appointed, so might they hope for a larger portion of His Spirit if they duly prayed for it, and were watchful. The power which remained with them was of two kinds, legal and moral; as ministers they might exercise such outward power as the law of Christ's Church gave them; and both as ministers and as men, their work would be blessed to God's glory and the salvation of their brethren in proportion to the measure vouchsafed them of the spirit of holiness or the spirit of wisdom. And so we doubt not that all faithful ministers of Christ's Church lawfully appointed to their ministry by those who have authority given them in their several congregations, will have " Christ" truly "with them, even unto the end of the world."

It shows how little the writer whom I am noticing is qualified to write upon such matters, when he says that " it would not materially alter the argument," though we suppose Christ's words to have been spoken not to the Apostles, but to the Church in general. According to his notion of the sense of the words as spoken to the Apostles, it would make the whole difference between a superstitious error and an important truth. For the question is, whether the Church has the power of ordination committed to it, to be vested in what hands she pleases, or whether one particular set of men hold it independent of the Church. Bishops ordaining as " the organs of the Church" constitute, as I believe, a Church Government most true in theory and most excellent in practice. Bishops ordaining in right of their apostolical descent, without reference to the authority of the Church, constitute a lame and inconsistent Popery, false in theory, and in practice inefficient.

In truth, however, it seems a narrow interpretation of Christ's promise either to understand it as addressed especially to the Apostles, or as having reference to the authority of Church government. It appears to be the general blessing given to that Universal Church, which, in the words immediately preceding, our Lord had contemplated as the fruit of His Apostles' labours. It was surely that great multitude whom no man could number, brought into the kingdom of God out of every race and language, baptized into the name and service of God, the Father, the Son, and the Holy Ghost, and walking in the ordinances of Christ their risen Lord, with whom Christ promised by His Spirit eternally to abide. And to limit this promise to the right of ordaining or ministering in the congregation, or to talk of it as addressed " to the episcopal body thus created, which is to last for ever," is like the profaneness which understood by the Church " against which the gates of hell should not prevail," " the Church acknowledging the authority of the successor of St. Peter," or which limits its meaning now, to " the Church which preserves the true apostolical succession of episcopacy."

Great stress has been laid on the following words from St. Paul in his second epistle to Timothy, ii. 2. " The things that thou hast heard of me among many witnesses, the same commit thou to faithful men who shall be able to teach others also." Let us consider the circumstances under which these words were written. In Ephesus and its neighbourhood, as in other places, there were growing up the most fearful corruptions of Christianity, partly in the form of superstition, partly in that of licentiousness, and partly of the two combined. The consequence was that, as St. Paul declares, " all those who were in Asia" (the Roman province so called) " were turned away from him." He therefore urges Timothy not only to exert himself vigorously to check all this evil, but to provide others, on whom he could depend, to assist him in the work. The teachers of error were busy; it became Timothy to oppose them by appointing teachers who would love and enforce the truth. This was the more necessary, inasmuch as it is probable that some of the elders of the Church of Ephesus[a] were themselves amongst the teachers of error, which would of itself be a reason why St. Paul should address himself particularly to Timothy and invest him with especial authority. We are not to suppose that in the first century of the Christian era all Christians acknowledged the authority of the Apostles, as it is universally recognised now. Humanly speaking, it was a struggle whether we should have Christianity, or whether Paganism was only to be supplanted by systems equally false and mischievous. How naturally in such a contest would the Apostles be anxious that those whom they ordained should themselves ordain others, to secure if possible, a succession of ministers who should retain the truth of the Gospel amidst the monstrous heresies which threatened to overwhelm it. And to any one who reads Clement's Epistle to the Corinthians attentively, it is evident that this is the cause of his insisting so earnestly on the apostolical succession of the Bishop of Corinth. It was to secure true and apostolical Christianity, by putting in the supreme government of the Church such men only as could be fully depended on

[a] [Acts xx. 30.]

for their attachment to the apostolical doctrine, and their knowledge of what that doctrine was. But this, which for one generation was a wise and most useful expedient, lost in the course of years both its necessity and its efficacy. Those who had lived with the Apostles might represent their principles faithfully in the main, however mixed with some errors of their own; but the disciples of these disciples of the Apostles retained the impression much more faintly and incorrectly, and in every succeeding age the security would be less and less, till at length it would vanish altogether. On the other hand, it was mercifully ordered by God's providence, that as the personal and traditionary memory of the apostolical doctrine wore out or became corrupted, so all who called themselves Christians came to acknowledge the authority of the Apostles, and to refer to their written memorials as to a certain standard of divine truth. Thus on the one side the Scriptures became universally allowed as an authority, while on the other the possibility of preserving Christian doctrine uncorrupted by mere personal recollection or tradition became continually more hopeless. The apostolical succession, most essential so long as it was confined to the period when the Apostles were personally remembered, and when another ministry not acknowledging the apostolical authority was striving for ascendancy in the Church of Christ, became an unmeaning name, so soon as they who called themselves the Apostles' successors had no better means of knowing their intentions and principles, and no greater inclination to follow them when known, than the general body of Christian believers. The paramount and exclusive authority of the New Testament, which would endure throughout all ages, came happily in the place of an authority of tradition, whose nature was essentially perishable. So that here, as in so many other instances, what was begun in most needful wisdom was continued out of habit, and perpetuated out of folly or fraud. The apostolical succession, which in the days of Clement of Rome was a most beneficial reality, was in the time of Cyprian become a phantom, and from that time onwards sunk more and more into a fond and pernicious superstition.

Be it again remembered, that the superstition consists not in giving the preference to an episcopal government, nor in feeling delight in the associations of antiquity with which it is connected;—but in insisting upon it as necessary, and in supposing that what is called apostolical succession is a transmission of any of the extraordinary gifts enjoyed by the Apostles. This is a superstition, and has the true character of all superstition, presumption, uncharitableness, and practical uselessness. Nothing is more ennobling, when rightly taken, than to be descended from an illustrious ancestry; but when men consider their nobility to be in itself a virtue, and that they inherit the merits of their forefathers by the mere circumstance of being born of their race, then what was elevating and improving becomes at once foolish and mischievous.

* * * * * *

APPENDIX III.

LETTER I.

TO CHEVALIER BUNSEN.

[This is the first and only letter of a series, commenced apparently in 1839-40, about the same time as the Fragment at the beginning of this volume. See Letters to Mr. Marshall and Archdeacon Hare, January and October, 1840. (Life and Correspondence, 4th Ed. vol. ii. pp. 190. 233.) Although in substance the same as the preceding Fragments, yet it seemed not out of place here, as containing a brief summary of the Author's whole view of the subject.]

MY DEAR FRIEND,

I ADDRESS these letters to you, not only because the subject of them is one in which we both feel so deep an interest, and which we have so often discussed together both in conversation and in our letters, but also because your name will serve as an assurance to many that they need not fear to read what I have written;—and still more, because the thought of addressing you will at once animate me and make me careful whilst I am pursuing my work;—it will animate me, because I know that there will be much in it in which you will heartily sympathize;—it will make me careful, because there are some points on which we differ, and wherever this is the case, I well know that nothing but the fullest inquiry and most earnest thought would justify me in maintaining an opinion in opposition to yours.

Let me say at once, that in the following letters my endeavour will be to arrive at the perfect theory or idea of Church and State, such as they may one day be actually, and such as we should earnestly desire to see them. But it may be that they never can be such universally, and that within no definite period will they be perfectly such anywhere. Still if we have got the true and perfect model, our attempts to copy it may approach at last infinitely near to it; and even now, in our own lifetime, some results may be obtained, if men begin to work steadily in the right direction, instead of doing nothing, or moving at hap-hazard, or going deliberately wrong.

The philosophers of the ancient world, seeing the perverse state of things around them, delighted in conceiving the theory of a perfect commonwealth,—not in the fond hope of seeing it at once or entirely reduced to practice; but because they knew that law and government were according to their nature the mightiest instruments for the improvement of mankind; and yet, according to their actual state, were most opposed to it. The power by which alone the wall could be built was actually employed in raising it;—it was most to be desired, then, if they could stay it from doing mischief, and convert its influence into good:—it might not and would not work for good with the whole force which it possessed, or in the best direction; yet still it might be brought to work for the attainment of its proper object, instead of neglecting it, or even opposing it.

But we see two powers, each capable of doing great good separately, but when combined, fitted to do the greatest good which we can either conceive or desire. Both have done good separately, that is, when each was working without any consciousness, so to speak, of the existence of the other. But when made aware of each other's presence, and each coming within the sphere of the other's influence, then, unless their mutual relations be properly adjusted, they embarrass and injure each other's efficacy. Then, if they are not combined, they run counter to one another, and each becomes corrupted. It is of the greatest importance, therefore, to discover the true theory of their union, even though we may never be able to effect it perfectly in practice. We may prevent much mischief and do much good, even though after all there should be some mischief left which practically we cannot hinder, and some good which we find it impossible to attain.

The State and the Church were reared apart from each other, but each was fitted to receive its utmost perfection only in union with the other. After a time they met, but there were obstacles to their being properly united. Still, as if feeling that they were framed for each other, they have gone on restlessly working, always attempting to fulfil their destiny, but always finding that their neighbourhood to each other led to collision rather than union. And now, tired of their unsuccessful attempts, each in despair would abandon the other altogether, and try to seek its own happiness alone. Yet it was a true instinct which brought them together;—they are designed by God to be one. And if we can clearly point out the misunderstandings that have perplexed them, and the treachery which under a show of friendship has beguiled them, may we not hope that even yet they will reject the thought of utter separation, that even in their age they may at last find that appointed end of their being, which they should have attained in their early youth, had not their misfortune and their fault together so long delayed it?

The confusion and perversion of their relations appears to me to be clearly traceable to the one or the other of the two following propositions, or to the influence of both of them together.

1st. That the true Church of God is a society governed by bishops appointed in an unbroken succession from the Apostles: that these bishops hold their power by Divine right, and that none but they, and subordinately the priests or presbyters appointed by them, have a right to rule in the Church;—and that farther, in these bishops and presbyters so appointed, and by virtue of their lineal succession from the Apostles, there resides a spiritual and priestly power;—that they may absolve Christians from their sins or refuse them absolution;—and that their ministry is essential in order to give to the sacraments their efficacy;—that where they do not minister, no spiritual benefit is imparted either by Baptism or the Lord's Supper;—and that where they minister, and through a certain virtue attached by God to their ministry, the water in Baptism and the bread and wine in the Communion acquire a superhuman efficacy, so as to convey spiritual blessings to those who receive them, unless there is any positive and wilful sin in the recipient which destroys in his particular case, at least to a certain degree, the virtue of the sacrament.

2nd. That the State or civil society has for its principal, if not for its only object, the providing for the security of men's bodies and goods:—that therefore religion as such is out of its province,—and that it has no right to interfere with only spiritual matters. This doctrine, in order to be consistent, should maintain farther that the State has nothing to do with any moral matters, except so far as they may affect the bodies and goods of its people;—but its advocates shrink generally from avowing this conclusion,—and thereby they cut away the ground from under their feet, and can only justify their exclusion of religion from the care of the State on the supposition that religion is not moral, but merely ritual and mystic, or theoretical;—a supposition which has in fact been greatly countenanced by the language and practice of those who have held the first mentioned doctrines with regard to the Church.

Thus, while the first doctrine demoralizes the idea of the Church by making it a system ritual rather than moral, and mystic rather than spiritual, so the second doctrine demoralizes the idea of the State, by making it a contrivance for man's physical welfare only. And thus the Church and State, which if the true moral character of each be upheld are perfectly identical, are necessarily separated when each is made to assume a false and unworthy character, of superstition on the one hand, and of the lowest worldliness on the other. Nor is it necessary that both these doctrines should be held at once in order to destroy the true relations of Church and State; for the prevalence of either one of them is sufficient to effect it. Where the most just and elevated notions of the purposes and duties of civil society are entertained, the false doctrines with respect to the Church are a bar to the identification of the two societies in one, because they involve a system of priestcraft, which is incompatible with all good government, and with the moral and spiritual improvement of mankind. And where the character and duties of the Church are most truly apprehended, still if men conceive of the State as of a contrivance only for the security of body and goods, the Church could not identify itself with such a society without apostacy.

Thus Mr. Gladstone, in his recent work on " The State in its Relations with the Church," while he entertains the most just and comprehensive notions of the end and duties of civil society, yet appears to regard the Church as a society with a divinely appointed government of its own, deriving its powers from a source higher than human law, and therefore not amenable to any government founded merely upon law, but capable of forming an alliance with the State, as one sovereign power with another. " The Church," says he, " professes to be an institution not deduced by human reason from any general declaration of God's will, but actually and (so to speak) bodily given by God, founded through His direct inspiration, and regularly transmitted in a divinely appointed, though human line;" p. 66. " It is a system," he goes on, " to which the State has itself yielded faith and homage, as of divine authority." Clearly then the divine must not yield to the human, and either the Church and the State must remain perpetually distinct, or else the forms of the latter, which are confessedly human and changeable, must give place to those of the former, claiming as they do the sanction of divine right, and Christians must be governed either by a Pope, or by a council or synod of Bishops.

On the other side there are many, the able reviewer of Mr. Gladstone's work in the Edinburgh Review being of the number, who see that the divine right of bishops is precisely on a level with that of kings, or parliaments, or the popular assemblies of a pure democracy:—that the notion of an indefeasible succession of ministers, deriving their power from their succession, is wholly unfounded and mischievous, even if these ministers are considered merely in the light of governors:—but that in fact the doctrine of succession is based upon the supposition that these ministers are priests, and possess certain mystical powers as such;— and that so regarded it is not simply mischievous, but

G

is eminently false and even contradictory to Christianity, forming a system wholly at variance with and essentially destructive of Christ's religion and Church. But unhappily these same persons hold the doctrine that the State has only to provide for men's bodies and goods;—and thus they also render the identification of Church and State impossible; they assign to the greatest power upon earth objects so secondary, that when raised to this disproportionate eminence, they are actually evil;—for he who gives to the sovereign power of law no better purpose than the checking wrong offered to body and goods, encourages the opinion that body and goods are the most precious things in the world, since they are the exclusive object of what is confessedly the most comprehensive of human societies,—and the first in rank and in power.

By God's blessing we in England have recognised, although rather by a providential overruling of our purposes than from a consciousness on our part of its full value, that great doctrine which is at once negative and positive; which, not content with denying and exposing falsehood, offers to us in the place of the falsehood so destroyed that divine truth in which is contained all goodness. This doctrine is that of the King's Supremacy;—which while it puts downs the false claims of the pretended apostolical succession on the one hand, denies no less firmly on the other hand the notion that the State has only to look after men's bodies and goods. It declares the identity of the Church and State, when each has attained to its perfection; both desire to effect man's greatest good; but the Church during her imperfect state is deficient in power;—the State in the like condition is deficient in knowledge:—one judges amiss of man's highest happiness; the other discerns it truly, but has not the power on a large scale to attain it. But when blended into one, the power and knowledge become happily united; the Church is become sovereign, and the State has become Christian.

Historically, as you well know, the second of the two false principles mentioned above is but a recent reaction against the evil consequences of the first. It is so recent, that hazardous as it may be to assert a negative, we might, I believe, safely challenge any one to show that it existed in its complete and developed form before the eighteenth century. The germ of it, no doubt, existed much earlier, and is contained in fact in the assumptions of the first false principle. But that first false principle is all but coeval with the origin of Christianity; it has obtained such a hold on men's minds and on their language, that even in later days, when its practical results excited the liveliest opposition, men have rather tried to neutralize its evil by setting up that contrary and no less mischievous error about the exclusively physical objects of political society, than they have laid the axe to the root, and hewn down the poison tree which has not only cumbered but has tainted as with an influence of death the ground of Christ's vineyard. Yet once remove this first error, and all temptation to maintain the second vanishes;—once connect the Church with notions of free and just government, and no one would ever dream of restricting the care of such a government to the lowest part of our compound nature, our bodies, and our external welfare.

It is more satisfactory in all things to be constructive rather than destructive. Instead, therefore, of attacking in the first instance the two errors which have been noticed as interfering with the perfect developement of Christ's Church, we will rather suppose them to have no existence, and exhibit the Church as it would or might be, if neither of these errors interfered with it. In other words, we will suppose the doctrine of the King's Supremacy to be worked out to its proper conclusions, unembarrassed by the doctrines of Laud and his party on the one hand, or by those of Warburton and some modern writers who hold similar sentiments on the other. " Formam quidem ipsam et tanquam faciem honesti videbis, quæ si oculis cerneretur, mirabiles amores excitaret sui."

[It may here be well to refer finally to the other parts of the Author's published works in which the subject of the preceding Fragments is treated. The theory of the identity of Church and State is set forth in the Postscript to the " Principles of Church Reform," and the " Letters on Church and State " in the " Herts Reformer," (Miscellaneous Works.) That part of it which more especially relates to the State, is treated more at length in the " Christian Duty of conceding the Roman Catholic Claims," the Preface to the third volume of the Edition of Thucydides, and in the " Inaugural Lecture," and the Sixth of the " Lectures on Modern History;" Sermons, vol. ii. (the 29th to the 33rd); vol. iv. (the 39th and 40th); vol. vi. (the 7th in Appendix I.) That which relates to the Church, in Sermons, vol. iii. (the 11th and 20th, and Appendix I.); vol. iv. (the Introduction, with the 24th, 28th, 29th, 30th, and 38th.]

THE END.

G. Woodfall and Son, Printers, Angel Court, Skinner Street, London.

www.ingramcontent.com/pod-product-compliance
Lightning Source LLC
Chambersburg PA
CBHW021808230426
43669CB00008B/668